Double, double, toil and trouble;
Fire burn and housing bubble.

Contents

Introduction 5

Chapter 1
Home Prices 10
Mortgage Rates 13
Affordability 16
Inventory 17
Sales 23
Policy 24
Federal Reserve Bank 26
Quantitative Easing (QE) 29

Chapter 2
Psychological Impact 33
Defining Affordability 35
True Cost of Homeownership 38
Cost to Build 39
California 41
Hawaii 43
Homelessness 45
Institutional Investors 47
Foreign Buyers 51
Conclusion 54

Chapter 3
Sector Behemoth 59
National Association of Realtors (NAR) 61
Controlling the Narrative 63
Housing Indicators 67
Valuation 68
Fundamental Valuation 72

New Technology 77
Valuation Example 79

Chapter 4
Quiz 88
Confirmation Bias 91
Anchoring Bias 93
Herding 95
Over-Confidence 96
Self-Attribution 97
Over-Optimism 98
Conclusion 100

Chapter 5
Government Intervention 103
Public Housing 106
Crisis in the Making 107
Housing and the Economy 109
History Repeats Itself...111

Chapter 6
Cycles 118
Technical Analysis 121
Fundamental Analysis 125
Rent vs Buy 128

Epilogue 131

Useful Websites 133
References 135
Index 143

Disclaimer: The information contained in this book and references to other resources are not intended as, and shall not be understood, or construed as advice. I am not a real estate advisor, nor am I holding myself out to be, and the information contained in this book is not a substitute for advice from a professional agent who is aware of the facts and circumstances of your situation. I have endeavored to ensure the information provided in this book and the resources mentioned are accurate and useful. Regardless of anything to the contrary, nothing in this book should be taken as a firm recommendation. Choices regarding transactions in real estate remain the responsibility of the individual.

Copyright © 2024 by Victor Saumarez

All rights reserved. No part of this publication may be reproduced, distributed, or transmitted in any form or by any means, including photocopying, recording, or other electronic or mechanical methods, without the prior written permission of the author, except in the case of brief quotations embodied in critical reviews and certain other noncommercial uses permitted by copyright law.

Introduction

What is wrong with the real estate market? Why are homes so expensive, and why are there so few homes for sale, especially it seems in the post-COVID era? It's clear fewer homes means higher prices. What is puzzling, though, is home prices have continued going up despite mortgage rates being higher. That can only mean supply is too low to satisfy even the muted demand imposed by higher mortgage rates.

At the time of writing in 2024, the reason often cited for the lack of supply is because there are not enough new homes being built. While that is undeniably true the problem is more complex. Other reasons given for the lack of supply are that many retirees don't want to downsize preferring to stay put. In fact, many other homeowners simply can't afford to move due to the higher mortgage rates. This is often referred to as the 'lock-in' effect. These taken together are what distinguish the current crisis from the one in 2006, which was initially explained by so-called 'subprime' lending. Lenders had relaxed their lending criteria considerably. Easy access to credit increased demand for homes as more and more people qualified for a mortgage.

As long as home prices continued to climb lenders were comfortable that their collateral was secure. The error in judgment was that many maintained home prices only ever go up as they indeed had done in previous decades. But when prices became unsustainable—as they do in bubbles—the house of cards came tumbling down creating a credit crisis and a global recession.

The 2006 crisis had clear causes. The post-covid crisis has different causes. What they share in common is very lofty prices and to a lesser degree a sensitivity to interest rates. A decades-long period of declining interest rates has coincided with a dramatic increase in the value of homes. It was almost as if home prices were behaving like bond prices. The analogy is useful because bonds and homes share some traits. Bonds have an inverse relationship with interest rates. As interest rates go down, their value goes up and vice versa. This is because a bond's price is linked to the interest it pays out. Homes don't produce interest payments, but their prices can be linked to incomes. This is certainly true for commercial real estate. The higher the income the greater the price. Similarly, the greater the purchasing power due to lower borrowing costs the more it chases up prices. This all points to the outsized role central banks play in the housing market. It is these powerful institutions, it should be noted, which pull the levers that control interest rates that affect mortgage rates.

Many will ask why all this matters since higher home values are good for homeowners because they create wealth and provide a much-needed buffer in retirement. Moreover, this all has to be good for the economy, yes? After all, housing comprises a large chunk of GDP. All things being equal these arguments have merit. In other words, if home prices conform to the fundamentals of affordability there shouldn't be a problem. However, when large sections of the population can't afford to buy a home then problems start and only get worse when temporary fixes are applied. These usually come in the form of interest rate tinkering and lowering barriers to borrowing.

The fix never comes in the form of allowing prices to correct fully. One explanation for this might be fear. To allow market forces to do their bidding could have inestimable, catastrophic consequences for individuals and the economy. Falling home values lead to foreclosures, which impacts credit markets and businesses. This all played out after the 2006 housing bubble. Furthermore, the short-term nature of politics is geared towards palliatives, rarely cures. Fiscal and monetary stimulus, bailouts, and regulatory changes are the levers used to minimize the impact on the economy when unwieldy forces threaten to destabilize everything.

The problem with quick-fix measures is they often push the problem down the road. It is in this respect that the post-covid housing crisis is not occurring in isolation, but is a continuation of the prior housing crisis that was never allowed fully to play out. This matters because when prices recover too quickly the likelihood of them getting out of control again increases. And this is exactly what has happened. The consequences of an over-valued residential housing market include a widening wealth gap, slowing household formations, homelessness, affordability issues, foreclosures, equity destruction, discontentment, uncertainty, and ultimately economic deterioration.

Answers to questions about what's wrong with the housing market are not straightforward. If they were, solutions would have been found. To blame monetary policy alone obscures the wider picture. The way homes are valued, the commission-driven model used to buy and sell homes, NIMBY-ism, zoning restrictions, fiscal policy, demographics, the commoditization of homes as investments, herd behavior, information asymmetry, and even climate change have their roles to play in shaping real estate dynamics.

Housing woes aren't unique to the US, or even the so-called developed economies. If we extrapolate common symptoms felt in different parts of the world it helps determine the most likely causes. China has encouraged developers to build on an unimaginable scale. Poor planning and conception have led to the emergence of ghost cities, where block after block of new homes sit vacant. Canada, Sweden, and Turkey have their own demons. Vancouver home prices reached stratospheric levels. Each country will have idiosyncratic problems associated with housing, but the last two decades have taught us global economic interconnectedness can have globally systemic consequences. But how is it that local housing problems are mirrored simultaneously in different corners of the world?

If we narrow down our focus we see 'all roads lead to Rome'. The US dollar is the dominant currency in the world and when the US lowers interest rates many countries are compelled to follow suit.

Chapter 1

This can't be right!

Home Prices

The Joint Center for Housing Studies of Harvard University published a report entitled 'The State of the Nations Housing 2023'. Findings show many more recent problems with housing, especially those affected by the pandemic outbreak COVID-19. In particular, millions of potential home-buyers were priced-out of the housing market as prices and the cost burden of homeownership significantly increased. The initial run-up in prices was followed by a softening as these costs cooled demand. However, an affordability crisis had become more visible.

The report points to a pent-up demand from millennials keen to form households dating back to 2017, boosted by federal stimulus, student loan payment suspensions, increased savings, and later the need for larger spaces as the pandemic hit. By 2022, this demand eased as it was largely satisfied and as costs increased with rising mortgage rates and other home-related expenses.

The report expands into areas such as racial segregation, under-investment in existing stock, demographic shifts, climate change, and challenges faced by developers. Overall, the picture painted is one of a housing market facing steepening challenges and a glib outlook. However, the most pressing of issues is affordability, because it lies at the heart of most of what is wrong with the housing market in modern times. A good starting point, therefore, is with home prices and their seemingly incessant gravity-defying upward momentum. It is both baffling and worrying.

When we look at home price charts the housing market seems to resemble an art auction out to lunch with the stock market. Why is this happening? To answer this question you need to trace the history of the housing market from 2006 to 2024. During this period more than any other, home prices have shown a remarkable capacity to rise to levels that seem at odds with the ability of many to pay for them.

The graph below shows the Case Shiller Home Price Index from the 1980s to early 2024. The shape of the graph speaks volumes. From January 2012 to January 2024, home prices climbed 57% nationally and were 42% higher in 2024, than their 2006 peak. Adjusted for inflation the number is less, but it is still above the

2006 level. Starting in 2020, the graph shows prices accelerated, then fell for a brief period in 2022 and early 2023, before picking up again. The fall was particularly prevalent in over-heated markets such as Boise and the Bay Area where prices fell well into double digits.

Case Shiller Home Price Graph

Source: Standard & Poor Corelogic

Large regional differences, also a feature of the 2006 bubble, illustrate that national housing statistics are more useful to economists and policy-makers seeking an overall picture. Real estate is local with some states and urban centers displaying a remarkable capacity to buck the national trend. According to the Case Shiller Metropolitan Home Price Index more recent regional differences were significantly greater than in 2006. This may be a result of 2024 nominal home prices being much higher than in 2006. It is important to note the index calculates price changes using repeat sales as opposed to the median or the mean home price and then averages three months. This is thought to be a more accurate measure of home price movement.

Although home prices display regional differences, the housing market as a whole is interconnected by lenders and GSEs, which underwrite mortgages. This is why in 2006, the credit crisis was systemic reaching even into other countries that had invested in MBSs (mortgage-backed securities). The important point here is regional housing market dynamics are not contiguous. In fact, pricing can be exported across state lines as homeowners from more expensive states sell and move to cheaper states pushing up local home prices.

Mortgage Rates
Home prices are only one side of the equation. On the other side sits mortgage rates, which have a quasi-inverse relationship to price. This relationship is not tightly correlated as there is a lag between the two. In principle, if one goes down the other goes up. Lower interest rates mean higher home prices and vice versa. To see this relationship in action you need to go back in time. From as far back as the 1980s, mortgage rates have declined consistently over four decades. In 1981, they were around 18%, and in 2020 they had dropped precipitously to 2.7%. The reason they were so high in the 1980s had to do with radical steps taken by the Federal Reserve Bank to control rampant inflation. However, if we go back to the early 1970's, mortgage rates have averaged 7.7% over a 50-year period.

Median home prices in 1981 were about $60,000, which is about $210,000 in today's money. The Federal Reserve Bank of St Louis shows the median price of a US home in the first quarter of 2024 was $420,800. To put this into a regional context, the median price of a home in California was double the national level for the same period. The median household income nationally was about $78,000 in early 2024, which puts the median-priced home out of reach for most conventional mortgages with a 20% down payment. For California, it is estimated only about 15% of the population can afford the median-priced home in 2024. Estimates of median household income vary wildly, but for a home priced at $875,000 monthly mortgage payments are nearly $5,000, which needs roughly $180,000 annual income to service. Even with small percentage differences in estimates, these numbers are a cause for concern.

From the mortgage graph below it can be seen that mortgage rates declined for four consecutive decades, in contrast to home prices that have risen. While there remains some debate about the correlation between prices and mortgage rates, conventional wisdom says a cheaper cost to borrow would increase demand for homes. Increased demand pushes up the price of any commodity. However, while mortgage rates jumped sharply from 3.2% in January 2022 peaking at 7% towards the end of that year, home prices declined but then picked up, even though mortgage rates remained elevated.

Mortgage graph

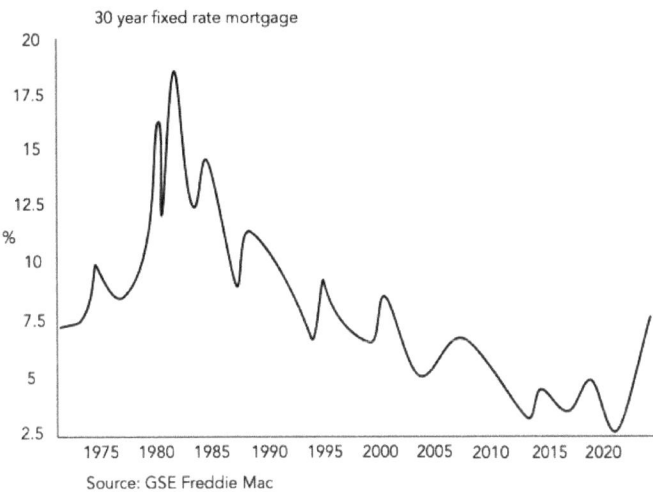

Sometime during the spring of 2023, there was a reversal of fortunes. While home price declines were not widely advertised the seasonal spring bounce that immediately followed was touted as a 'recovery' in the media and remarkably the momentum continued. This was puzzling as data were screaming the reverse should be happening. Not only were prices rising, but bidding wars were being widely reported. It seems inconceivable that anyone would over-bid, in an over-bought market, that was already over-valued, but that is what was happening.

Affordability

Affordability as measured by income-to-price appeared to be at breaking point. This affordability crisis has been especially acute in California, Hawaii, and other coastal areas. The California Association of Realtors released startling numbers that claim only

15% of Californians could afford the median-priced home in 2023, which stood at $834,600. Incomes clearly had not been keeping pace with prices, yet the diminishing number of homes for sale was still managing to find buyers. Demand, although tempered by higher rates, was still there. What was driving this demand from buyers is unclear. It may simply be supply was so drastically low, it was unable to satisfy even muted demand. The result was increasing home prices and worsening affordability.

In 2022, home prices in the US were 5.6 times higher than the median income. In several markets, it was as high as 8 times higher, and in California and Hawaii, home prices were an astounding 12 times median incomes. The norm in prior decades hovered around 3 times the median income. Between 2019 and 2022, home prices outgrew incomes by a factor of 6. Incomes were not only not keeping pace with home prices, they seemed to be completely detached from them. This is an unmistakable sign that things had gotten very out of hand with housing.

Despite the demand-supply imbalance, the axiom there are buyers in every market holds, and nowhere is this more true than in California. Higher earners and a migration of wealthier, cash-rich buyers might explain how such high prices are supported. Buyers from New York and San Jose to less expensive locations in California, or other states may also explain some of the apparent willingness to over-pay. Californians selling up and moving to Florida or Texas can buy more house and at a lower price, pushing up prices and pricing-out local residents.

Low Inventory
The graph below shows a very clear downward trend in active listings of homes for sale from 2017 to 2022. From 2022, there was a small uptick in inventory, but it was still well below the level it needed to be for prices to normalize. According to Redfin, an online home listing service, the trough in months supply was in December 2021, when months supply was a little over one month. Months supply is the amount of time it would take to sell all listed homes at the current sales rate. One month's supply is a critically low level, well below the six-month supply needed for supply and demand equilibrium.

Harvard University's 2023 State of the Nation's Housing report explains the lack of supply in terms of years of declining construction, demographic shifts, a disincentivized seller's market as a result of higher rates and fewer purchase options. The vast majority of mortgages had a rate of 3-4%, which almost doubled in 2023. The report goes on to state the pick-up in inventory was a result of homes sitting for longer on the market as opposed to more new listings. Homes had been sitting on the market for a median of 65 days in early 2023. Redfin claims this number was actually a little above 50 days, and dropped significantly to 35 days by April 2024.

It is interesting to note that while re-sales of existing homes dropped dramatically, the slack was picked up by new construction, which reached record levels as a percentage of overall supply. It is estimated that over 30% of homes for sale were newly constructed homes in 2023. Nevertheless, sales of both existing homes and new homes remained in decline.

Active Listings (Inventory) Graph

Source: Realtor.com

Given the lion's share of inventory is re-sales, as opposed to new homes, it begs the question of why homeowners were not selling. The popular suggestion is higher mortgage rates were a disincentive, since selling a home and then buying another, in most cases, means sacrificing 3-4% for a 6-7% mortgage rate. A working paper published in March 2024, by the Federal Housing Finance Agency (FHFA) titled 'The Lock-In effect of Rising Mortgage Rates' concludes:

> *[F]or every percentage point that market mortgage rates exceed the origination interest rate, the probability of sale is decreased by 18.1%. This mortgage rate lock-in led to a 57% reduction in home sales with fixed-rate mortgages in 2023 Q4 and prevented 1.33 million sales between 2022 Q2 and 2023 Q4. The supply reduction increased home prices by 5.7%, outweighing the direct impact of elevated rates, which decreased prices by 3.3%.*

In other words, higher mortgage rates mean less homes for sale, and that pushes up prices more than the increased cost to borrow pulls down prices. The paper goes on to state that had the lock-in effect not happened there would have been 1.33 million more homeowners. In other words, more people would have been able to buy a home. Interestingly, higher mortgage rates affect expensive homes more. A $600k home is nearly twice as unlikely to be listed for sale than a home half the price, possibly because the owners can afford to wait for a more opportune time to sell. However, this doesn't play out across some ethnic groups which are more sensitive to the lock-in effect.

Higher LTVs (Loan-to-value), the size of a loan compared to price, is not a factor in how sensitive a home is to increasing mortgage rates. The paper concludes, that since the lock-in effect increases as mortgages are closer to being paid off, we can't expect much to change in terms of supply. While these findings are compelling, there wasn't much evidence to show whether other factors may also be influencing decisions to sell, such as the desire to stay put and retire in place. And how do you account for the 40% of mortgage-free homeowners? The lock-in effect is only going to influence borrowers.

Finding a home when choice is so limited is certainly a challenge, whether a mortgage is needed, or not. At first glance, the inventory dilemma would seem at odds with demographic trends. Since boomers own 27% of homes, the expectation is most of these homes will be coming onto the market as the aging population downsizes. However, this doesn't appear to be happening despite 2024 being a record year for retirement dubbed the 'silver tsunami' by the AARP.. The reasons for this are a little less clear but are probably mostly to do with economics and emotions. For example, it is estimated well over half of retirees do not have sufficient pension provisions, to meet their needs in retirement with social security only supplying about 40% of income. For many, home equity is the larger part of their total assets. Herein lies the paradox.

Homes don't normally contribute to income. Many boomers don't want to sell their homes, thereby releasing home equity to boost income shortfalls in retirement. Ploughing realized home equity gains into alternative investments such as annuities, or other fixed-income products doesn't enter the calculation for many. Financial markets are viewed as being too risky, unsuitable, or too complex. Fears of income shortfalls in retirement have compelled 20% of boomers to continue working to the age of 70, and beyond.

While individual circumstances will vary considerably, it may be argued a golden opportunity is being squandered. Home equity gains have never been as high and fixed-income products are offering yields not seen for two decades. The opportunity cost of not realizing home equity gains is significant. Financial behaviorists are likely having a field day with this 'cognitive error'. In fairness, personal circumstances vary so downsizing is not necessarily for everyone, and not everyone needs, or would benefit from unlocking home equity gains.

For many, downsizing from what is already a modest home creates little to no utility. For others with more secure assets, retiring in place may seem economically more feasible than living in elderly care facilities, which can be prohibitively expensive. Relying on family, friends and local support services in familiar surroundings becomes the logical choice. Other factors will also determine downsizing decisions. Some homeowners have taken out loans against their home equity tying them to repayments well into retirement. Ironically, many of these loans are to help children struggling with huge down payments for their own homes.

Naturally, many boomers want to pass on their homes to their children by way of inheritance, believing large home equity gains are cemented in for eternity. Other reasons for not selling homes might be sentimental, or other behavioral traits that will be gone into later in the book. In sum, the low supply of re-sale homes has its roots in a reluctance to sell. That reluctance may be dictated by personal circumstances and preferences, or be based on poor decision making. Again, we get back to the question of what will trigger a reversal prompting would-be sellers to market their homes.

As alluded to above, falling prices may create a panic to sell to realize gains. Another popular notion is a significant drop in mortgage rates will incentivize sellers. However, a lower cost to borrow would likely increase demand, and If supply doesn't increase with it the affordability crisis could worsen.

Sales
Notwithstanding the remarkable resilience of the housing market to absorb large changes in interest rates, an external shock or recession would likely bring about a needed correction in prices. Some economists predicted a recession as early as the 4th quarter of 2024. LEIs (leading economic indicators) produced by The Conference Board, a widely followed think tank, did not, however, forewarn an imminent recession in its May 2024 report. Given the anticipated interest rate cuts in the latter part of the year, it would seem the economic cycle will enter a cooling period with a contraction in growth that normally follows.

Sales volume is an important indicator for where the housing market is heading. According to the MLS

(Multiple Listing Service), which compiles data relating to residential real estate, home sales have dropped precipitously from a peak in October 2020 to February 2024. The 42% decline marks a level not seen since the depths of both the COVID-19 crisis and the 2009 financial crisis. The collapse in home sales follows the downward trend in inventory. Fewer homes for sale normally means fewer homes are being sold. And given what we know about the reluctance of homeowners to sell, it's not surprising new home sales have gained ground in overall sales numbers. Much higher mortgage rates have also hurt sales. In late 2020, mortgage rates bottomed at 2.7%, which coincides with a peak in sales. As mortgage rates rose, sales of homes started to decline. Year-on-year to April 2024, sales volumes continued to decline.

There is little doubt that despite demand exceeding supply, affordability is weighing heavily on the housing market. In terms of price, however, there was no let up in prices, with the western region of the US showing an annual 10% appreciation in April 2024, This is confirmed by the Case Shiller National Home Price Index. The index lags by a few months but shows a clear indication of home price increases for the year ending February 2024. Declining sales therefore do not appear to be directly correlated to prices in the current environment. This might seem counterintuitive since slowing sales is normally associated with a slowing economy and decelerating prices. When home prices confound expectations it raises the question of whether prices are sustainable.

Policy

Lastly, it is important to place housing dynamics of the last two decades into a policy context. Policy in respect of housing falls into two categories: public policy with government agencies driving household growth, and monetary policy headed by central banks that set interest rates and influence debt markets such as mortgage lending.

The creation of GSEs (Government Sponsored Entities), which date back as far back as the early part of the last century, was mandated with encouraging homeownership. The two most commonly known GSEs are Fannie Mae and Freddie Mac, which deal with the residential mortgage market. They form part of successive government programs to encourage targeted borrowing by way of government-backed guarantees and buying mortgages from lenders. Essentially, they lubricate the mortgage business making it easier to borrow by removing some of the risk. This broadens the market allowing more diverse groups, especially lower-income households, to get on the property ladder and build intergenerational wealth through home equity. This is both good for the economy since real estate contributes significantly to GDP, and good for sentiment because people are more content when they feel wealthier. Homeownership after all is synonymous with the 'American Dream'.

More recently, however, the housing conveyor belt has suffered setbacks. During the 2008-09 credit crisis Fannie Mae and Freddie Mac got into severe financial difficulties as bonds held by them were impacted by non-performing loans caused by defaulting borrowers. Homeownership got ahead of itself as the expansion of collateralized mortgages found their way onto Wall Street. The hitherto self-regulating mortgage market found itself grappling with financial shenanigans. As a result, regulation tightened but the damage to both local and interconnected global economies led to drastic fiscal and monetary measures. Policies designed to rescue economies and restore faith in severely disrupted credit markets came from central banks in the form of lowering short-term interest rates and Quantitative Easing (QE) that involved buying massive amounts of bonds, flooding the economy with liquidity.

Federal Reserve Bank
A prolonged period of monetary easing has had a profound effect on asset values, including housing. It has probably indirectly increased home values more than any other factor. The Central Bank of the US, the Federal Reserve Bank, or the Fed for short, is a quasi-governmental body that guides all interest rates. Formerly, this was done by using a simple supply and demand mechanism to control money in the system. When the Fed buys government bonds it puts money in the economy. An abundance of money means a lower cost to borrow. When the Fed sells bonds the money supply is decreased, so money becomes scarcer and the cost to borrow goes up.

After the financial crisis in 2009, the Fed's old system for influencing interest rates became less effective.

The inter-bank overnight borrowing rate, known as the federal funds rate was almost zero, and reserves (essentially cash) were flooding the system. More was needed to be done to stimulate the faltering economy and prevent deflation. So, instead of buying and selling government bonds to control the money supply and influence rates, the Fed decided to pay interest on bank reserves held at the central bank. This ensures banks won't lend below that rate since it won't be worth their while. This has become the replacement tool for keeping the target rate on track and influencing the federal funds rate.

For other financial institutions, the Fed sells them government bonds and buys them back the next day. This is called a reverse repurchased agreement, or 'repo' for short. The institution earns interest on the overnight money it receives from the Fed. As with the reserve rate, institutions are unlikely to lend at a rate lower than what they receive from the Fed, which acts as a floor for short-term rates. The repo mechanism is a secondary tool to the reserve rate mechanism. The main takeaway is that asset prices, be they stocks, bonds, or houses, are sensitive to interest rates, which themselves are influenced by the federal funds rate. Longer terms rates used in mortgages adjust according to what the market perceives will happen to short-term rates down the road.

Despite these powerful tools, the 2009 financial crisis was so severe the Fed had to resort to even more extreme measures. This took the form of what is commonly known as quantitative easing, which is essentially large-scale bond buying by a central bank. According to a public education document published by the Fed titled, "The Fed Explained", the bond-buying spree was so intense that by 2014, its balance sheet had ballooned by a factor of 5 in the space of seven years totaling a whopping $4.5 trillion. To put that in perspective it was equivalent to a quarter of the gross output of the whole US economy.

If we turn back the clock to 2001, the US and the UK started monetary easing in response to the bursting of the 'tech bubble' when stock prices crashed. It is widely thought this laid the groundwork for the strong rise in share prices and the housing bubble in 2006. Fast forward to 2008, and the Fed embarked on the first phase of QE (quantitative easing). Japan was the first country to embark on QE, and both the UK and the Eurozone followed a similar path to the US. The US conducted three more QE operations with the final one being in 2020, in response to the economic slowdown caused by the pandemic. The period marks an important milestone in both housing and financial markets.

Two factors emerged that impacted asset values in ways not seen on such as scale. Firstly, the Fed had been buying MBSs (mortgage-backed securities), which had a direct impact on the housing market. It should be remembered that the Fed's dual mandate is primarily keeping unemployment and prices low. Secondly, markets became fixated on the Fed and its every move and utterance. This spawned the aphorism the 'Fed put', a reference to monetary policy providing a backstop to market volatility. Monetary easing was, de facto, expanding asset values in all classes. Further confirmation of this market dependency on the Fed was revealed by the so-called 'taper tantrum' that sent financial markets into a tailspin when the then Fed chair, Ben Bernanke, announced in 2013, that he was scaling back bond purchases. So important were Fed statements they became intrinsic to monetary policy under the banner of 'forward guidance'. Giving businesses and markets forewarning of future Fed actions would help everyone adjust thus reducing volatility in markets. So why is this relevant to housing?

Quantitative Easing (QE)
QE wasn't just the purchase of government debt, it extended into other types of securities. As mentioned above, one of those was mortgage-backed securities known simply as MBSs. These were held by GSEs, namely Fannie Me and Freddie Mac, that purchased mortgage debt from lenders to target lending operations to a wider demographic. Since both these entities were severely impacted by the 2008 credit crisis, the Fed stepped in to buy up their debt. This debt, in the form of collateralized mortgages, was repackaged and sold on to investors as fixed-income investments deriving their income from mortgage payments. The large-scale purchases of these securities not only helped support home prices, it also reduced mortgage rates encouraging borrowers to refinance.

While this helped by easing borrowing costs during a financially stressful period it also added the amount of debt with which homeowners were burdened. A theme was emerging that was becoming the go-to palliative for all debt-originated problems, viz., debt-oriented solutions.

Cheap debt encourages over-leverage, which increases sensitivity to interest rate changes and the risk of default. Simply adding more layers of debt magnifies these risks. That aside, MBSs had a role to play, principally that of broadening homeownership. Its goal was undoubtedly never to overburden the nation with debt. The other recurring theme exacerbating problems in the housing market is government proposals to backstop financial distress.

In late spring of 2024, Freddie Mac proposed guaranteed closed-end second mortgages to allow homeowners access to home equity, and to generate business for the lending industry. This would also release huge amounts of trapped equity into the economy. The potential downside is for those with little equity build-up, as default risk increases significantly if home prices fall. It is estimated that if Fannie Mae becomes involved in this scheme, the exposure to default risk increases exponentially. A similar theme played out in the 2006 housing crisis. Government intervention is often guided by political expediency and short-termism.

The guiding principle behind the Fed's purchases of MBSs was to encourage lending and increase aggregate demand. That is to say, its purpose was to stimulate the economy. To this day, there is much disagreement about how much—or even whether—QE had a positive impact in the way it was intended. There is much less disagreement, however, on its 'positive', but controversial impact on asset values including home prices. In the case of homes, intrinsic value was being obscured by an almost bond-like inverse relationship home prices were enjoying with low mortgage rates.

Homes were no longer just a roof over one's head with modest increases in value. They had taken on a new role. That new role was momentous wealth creation and a less risky substitute for financial investments. Ultimately, it offered a significant supplement to pensions that many feared would be inadequate to maintain a comfortable lifestyle in retirement. The paradox many homeowners fail to grasp is the wealth offered by ballooning home prices is trapped in home equity, an illiquid asset. Gains can only be realized by selling 100% of the home, a cumbersome process, and which many older homeowners don't want to do. Releasing home equity by borrowing against it merely adds to a homeowner's indebtedness. A home equity loan is often misleadingly described as 'releasing equity'. This is a misleading idea open to misuse as homeowners would use their homes as ATM machines.

The crucial point here is that the complex relationships between GSEs, lenders, mortgages, financial markets, home prices can all be distilled down to one element; the cost of debt, which is primarily influenced by central banks. Over the last four decades, we've seen interest rates decrease by a factor of seven, while home prices have increased over fivefold. Since incomes have not kept pace with these increases, value has become detached from the fundamentals.

The price of a home has become an afterthought, or appendage to the calculus, merely kowtowing to the debt overlord. The innate sense of value and intrinsic worth has been eroded and is fast becoming irrelevant. The housing market seems to be playing catch-up with an ever-changing landscape of false normals. Seeking justification for soaring home prices is drowned out by the overwhelming contentment felt by many as they marvel at new-found wealth captured in their homes. Affordability for many is merely a word, but for others, it's a harsh reality. It fosters divisions between generations, races, and income groups sowing the seeds for widening discontent.

Chapter 2

We need to hock grandma's old flatware!

This chapter will attempt to place the problems associated with the housing crisis into context. In a nutshell, high home prices have created a serious affordability dilemma. This is not helped by the wide range of affordability definitions. Nor is it helped by the fact attention has been focused on making homes affordable rather than what makes them unaffordable in the first place.

Psychological Impact
Real estate is a major component of economies so what impacts real estate will impact the economy. Likewise, changes in the economy can have consequences for well-being. Research suggests that emotional and physical well-being can suffer as a result of

financial stress. At the extreme, financial problems can lead to homelessness, which itself exacerbates health problems.

This problem is not exclusive to the US. Research around the world shows similar findings. For example, in Australia, a paper finds a link between financial hardship and mental health. Heavy housing costs affect both physical and mental health due to the stress of reduced income for important items such as food and medical care. Similar research has been conducted in Canada using a broad framework for viewing how high housing costs impact well-being and other social conditions. These include stress from financial insecurity to satisfy the most basic needs. In Toronto, nearly 30% of households spend more than the 30% affordability threshold, and a large percentage of those households spend up to 50% of income to keep a roof over their heads. It's been estimated the cost to the local economy was $37 billion in 2023, which is about the same amount spent on serious illnesses such as diabetes and cancer.

The problems associated with unaffordable housing go beyond health. As more and more people become negatively impacted by the financial stress of increasing costs of housing and the widening wealth gap that follows, social discontent festers and divisions within society widen. Movements such as populism arise out of such disaffection. While the exact origins of the Tea Party movement are in dispute, some say it started with a backlash to Barak Obama's 2009 Homeowners Affordability and Stability Plan.

The plan was aimed at preventing foreclosures by offering mortgage refinancing. A major criticism was it encouraged moral hazard by bailing out those involved in irresponsible mortgage lending and borrowing.

Defining Affordability
Affordability lies at the very heart of the current housing crisis. However, there is no universally agreed-upon definition, nor calculation for determining what is affordable. The consensus is no more than 30 percent of income should be spent on housing costs. There's some disagreement as to what expenses should be included, but it's a useful starting point for approximating what is affordable and what is not. On an anecdotal level, there is no doubt people are struggling to afford to buy or rent homes. At first glance, this would appear to be because housing costs have increased at a much faster pace than incomes. That is not so much because incomes have stagnated, which they have, but more because housing costs have exploded.

Home prices, mortgage payments, property taxes, insurance, and maintenance costs have risen so much and so quickly that they pose a serious financial burden, and no more so than in lower-income groups. Not having a universal definition and measure of affordability makes the task of providing support harder. Measuring median income against median house price has inherent problems. Many renters will earn lower incomes so cannot afford to buy a home. Some estimates put their number at 44 million in 2023, or

34% of all households. In urban centers that percentage will be much higher. The median income is, therefore, going to be skewed when measured against median home prices.

Some affordability measures don't take account of other costs such as property tax and insurance, which can vary wildly from state to state. Property tax in New Jersey is more than twelves higher than in Alabama. A think tank based in Washington DC, the Urban Institute, suggests only the incomes of renters who can afford to buy a home should be used to calculate affordability. The Institute points out that the affordability curve is steepest at lower income levels and along racial lines. People with higher incomes will have proportionately more disposable income despite higher home costs. This may in part be because wealthier households don't necessarily spend more on basic needs such as utilities and food, so have a cushion to budget more effectively when times are tough.

Comparing affordability across the nation, only 9% of renters can afford to buy in San Fransisco, whereas this number increases to 30% for Detroit. Since only 27% of renters can afford to purchase a home anywhere in the US, a large pool of households doesn't enter the homeownership affordability equation. It also sheds light on the growing wealth gap. Given the difficulties conceptually with affordability, care is needed when attempting accurately to describe instances of it. And the situation only seems to be getting worse.

One country seems to have an answer to the affordability crisis. That country is the Netherlands where 30% of housing is run by decentralized non-profit housing associations that build affordable homes. Rental income is used to maintain the properties and long-term loans used to fund new developments. The associations do not receive any direct government subsidies so are self-funding. Rents are considered comparatively low making them affordable to many on lower incomes. In 2022, a typical rent was around €763 a month. In addition, tenants enjoy robust protections of tenure and quality on a par with those in the private sector. That is not to say the Dutch don't have housing problems. In 2022, Bloomberg ranked the Netherlands 11th out of 30 OECD countries with housing markets at serious risk. Canada and Australia are in the top 5, and the US stole the number 7 spot. New Zealand was the star performer staking out the top position making it the most at-risk housing market in the ranking. New Zealand home price did fall 14% from their earlier peak, but despite the predictions, prices made a comeback in early 2024. This is similar to what happened in the US in 2022, with prices confounding expectations and defying the odds. Few had predicted an overheated market and a spike in mortgage rates would lead to higher prices. But that is exactly what happened.

True Cost of Homeownership
The main component of housing costs is debt servicing. In other words, the monthly interest and principal

payments on a mortgage. Other payments associated with housing include property tax, insurance, maintenance, and HOA fees more commonly found with condos and new homes. A consumer website calling itself Real Estate Witch estimated the actual overall cost of homeownership, including utilities, to be $18,000 in 2024. Maintenance and home improvement costs, however, were a big surprise for many first-time buyers. Altogether, costs are nearly 80% higher than many thought. Both property taxes and insurance costs have increased as a result of accelerating home values and structural damage from changing weather patterns.

These high costs impact affordability and lead to buyer remorse. Two-thirds of buyers said they regretted buying a home, saying it has hurt their personal finances and mental health. These extra costs have forced nearly 70% of homeowners to pay for them by going further into debt or dipping into savings. One of the most surprising findings is only 14% of homeowners thought buying was a good idea when home prices are lower. That may be because many young buyers believe home prices only ever appreciate, whereas they follow a cycle with peaks and troughs that have been growing in size in recent decades.

Home prices regionally vary considerably as do property taxes and insurance. New Jersey has by far the highest property tax, but the median price of a home in May 2024 was $536,200, which is above the national level at $439,716, but well below California at $860,500. With costs varying regionally, affordability is impacted differently. Where there is a convergence of high costs, such as in California, affordability concerns balloon.

Cost to Build
Given the variability of affordability regionally, there must be factors unique to some cities or states, that are absent in others. Generally, in rural areas where land is more abundant and incomes lower, homes are cheaper than in urban areas. This does not explain why home prices vary so much between cities and states. To help understand why this might be we need to look at what goes into building a home from conception to sale.

Two major components of a home's intrinsic value reside in the land it sits on and the cost to build, which includes material, labor, and profit. Two states, California and Hawaii, stand out as being the least affordable to live in due largely to these housing costs. Establishing the cost of land in either state is tricky. Using as an example of land zoned for residential development in Los Angeles, the price of an 8,000-square-foot lot can range from $20,000 to $1.5 million and sometimes higher. And this can all be within a few miles radius. The differences would appear to be due to what is going to be built on the land such as a single-family home, or a multi-family unit.

A similar picture emerges for Honolulu, where land is in short supply. However, neither Honolulu nor Los Angeles displays land prices that make them significant outliers compared with other major metropolitan areas. Miami, for example, has an exceptionally high price tag for land. Boise Idaho, has eye-watering land prices. It's not until you get to southern states that prices fall back to earth. So what other factors help explain why some cities and states have such expensive homes? Why are home prices and incomes needed to buy a home in California approximately twice what they are nationally?

The cost to build is going to be greater where labor costs are higher. Labor costs will be higher where the cost of living is greater and this factor accounts for the biggest regional variances in costs. Both California and Hawaii have high living costs, but the cost to build changes over time, so building a consistent picture is problematic. Also, most homes sold are resales and not new builds so construction costs only explain a portion of why home prices are high. It is likely new home prices will be determined by local market conditions. Developers will cost projects according to what a local market can bear. Land prices will also reflect the price developers are willing to pay to remain profitable. Given all the above factors, one is left with the conclusion that home prices in some states seem somewhat whimsical, and have become dislocated from the fundamentals.

California
Home prices are high in California in part because that is the expectation. Therefore, the willingness to pay lofty prices goes with the territory. Putting a price on a lifestyle is subjective and boils down to the will-

ingness of a buyer to pay it. Various behavioral traits influence buyers, and these will be explored in more detail in Chapter 4. Suffice it to say California has been successful in marketing itself as a desirable place to live. Given the affordability crisis in the state, some would say it's been too successful, and the premium paid is no longer commensurate with the lifestyle offered.

A deeper dive into the nuts and bolts of California's housing woes reveals a backdrop of well-meaning aspirations to build more homes and make housing more affordable, but which is all too often thwarted by competing interest groups. Pluralism is alive and well in California, but you can have too much of a good thing. Despite everything, it is ambitious to attempt any realistic numerical assessment of the effect of political wrangling on housing affordability. At best we can conclude the less that gets built as a result of resistance from various quarters, the greater the problem with affordability. However, the number of new homes being built has been increasing and comprises a greater part of total sales. Redfin puts that number at 30% in 2022. New homes tend to be more expensive than existing homes, which does fuel the affordability crisis. The relative costs to build around the country vary, but not as much as sales prices would suggest. Land prices thus look like a top contender for creating large regional price variations.

The non-profit online news organization, Cal Matters, claims 90% of Californians think home prices are a problem, and over 30% of residents are considering leaving the state, because of high living costs. This has led to California having the third lowest homeownership rate in the US. The state is home to seven out of ten cities with the highest number of rentals in the country, with San Fransisco leading the charge. One reason for this is that decreasing homeownership is driving would-be buyers into the rental market, where they are competing with people on lower incomes. This pushes up rents making them unaffordable to many on lower incomes.

Another major contributing factor driving up prices is local politics. Developers are faced with many hurdles before they can build enough homes to ease the dearth of supply. In 2020, there were many bills aimed at increasing supply, such as allowing higher-rise buildings to be built and curtailing environmental obstructions. However, none was passed. The idea was to increase density and build homes near public transport, a format that most big cities are familiar with. Objections centered on fears of gentrification, forcing out lower income groups, and destroying the character of neighborhoods by placing multistory homes next to single-family homes.

Demographics also play in role in the housing crisis. The population in California is growing faster than the rate of new homes being built. Moreover, only about 10% of homes being built are specifically designated as 'affordable'. Reduced funding has also set back affordable housing projects. The list goes on. California imposes prohibitively high fees on developers. Red tape, competing interests, and high costs don't augur well for the future of real estate in the Golden State. Estimates put the costs to the economy at hundreds of billions of dollars from lost consumption, lost construction, and homelessness.

So much money is tied up in real estate, putting so much at stake, that an unraveling would be painful and costly. Should that happen—and it may well do so—we can expect outsized government efforts to contain the problem over the short term, pushing the can yet further down the road. Moral hazard finds its way into every corner when governments fear retribution at the ballot box.

Hawaii
Hawaii is a unique case and being abundant in natural wonders there is some justification for higher prices based simply on desirability. Nevertheless, paradise needs workers to support its tourism industry, and they need somewhere affordable to live. According to the National Association of Realtors affordability index, Hawaii had an index rating of 53 in 2022. For a local housing market to be considered affordable, it needs an index number of 100. Hawaii is unaffordable, and this impacts locals disproportionately.

As with other states and cities, the situation became worse around the time of COVID-19 and mortgage rate increases. Monthly interest and principal payments for a typical mortgage went from $1,000 a month in 1987 to nearly $7,000 in 2023. The median price for a home in Honolulu eclipsed the $1 million mark in 2023. For three decades from 1990, home prices have increased almost at double the rate of wages. So, the affordability issue has been long in the making. Higher home prices push up rents as demand for rentals increases, which disproportionately affects those on lower incomes.

Honolulu has a serious homeless problem that is very much on display given the small size of the city. The cost of importing building materials, labor costs, land zoning restrictions, and land availability are all factors driving up the cost of new builds. Developers have been concentrating on building homes for the luxury market where profits are greater, at the expense of affordable homes. According to some accounts, in 2022 foreign investors are buying 2% of these luxury homes, 22% are being bought by out-of-state buyers, possibly as second homes. The remainder of the homes are being bought by local residents. A common complaint on the islands is that a lot of second homes exacerbate the shortage of homes for sale. Surprisingly, this is more of a problem for a dozen other states than it is for Hawaii, which may be due to very high home prices in the state.

Despite Hawaii's uniqueness and high desirability, the island chain shares similar intangible characteristics to California when it comes to home prices. Real estate is an important industry for both. Both states have been successful in nurturing desirability and lifestyle, to the extent it has created distortions in pricing, forcing many inhabitants living in either state to flee in search of more affordable living. For locals in

Hawaii who are forced to leave their ancestral lands, their plight is a bitter pill to swallow.

Homelessness

There is one very tangible consequence of the housing crisis that is both literally and figuratively a glaring blot on the landscape. Homelessness. It stands to reason that rapidly escalating home prices and rents will disproportionately affect people with lower incomes to the point many will fall off the housing ladder altogether and find themselves living rough on the streets. This is very unfortunate given its scale, and despite its high visibility, is an apparent blind spot with policymakers. There are very real sufferers and victims of this growing misfortune.

At the peak of the 2008 financial crisis, it was not uncommon to see the surreal spectacle of normal, middle-class Americans, having lost their homes, jobs, and savings living out of their cars. Thankfully, that situation was temporary for many. The more enduring aspect of homelessness has not receded, however. In fact, for many individuals, it has become worse. According to a report by the US Department of Housing and Urban Development (HUD), 653,104 people experienced homelessness in 2023. The increases became worse due to Covid-19, but also because of the affordability crisis in housing. The situation is especially acute for the 'unsheltered' who are living on the streets. Between 2022 and 2023, their ranks swelled by 11 percent. Many who served in the armed forces have also found themselves without anywhere to live.

Another worrying trend is many young people are now finding themselves in the same boat.

In California, where the homelessness problem is very concerning, 161,548 people were said to be homeless in 2020, while in Los Angeles that number was 90,000. By 2023, the number of homeless in California increased to 181,399 souls. One problem policymakers are having is knowing how much funding to allocate. The because data collection concerning the effectiveness of local government measures is a challenge. Given the lack of robust data on the numbers of homeless people, it is difficult to say with any degree of accuracy to what extent the problem is a direct result of the affordability crisis. Despite these difficulties, anecdotal evidence is abundant. News stories flood the airwaves of cities blighted by the problem of homeless people falling prey to crime, drugs, and illness from unsanitary conditions.

Institutional Investors
There has been wide speculation that institutional and foreign investors have had an impact on housing affordability in the US. After the housing crisis that started in 2006, it is estimated that 3.8 million people lost their homes to foreclosure. That transmutes to as many homes being temporarily removed from the market. In 2012, the FHFA (Federal Housing Finance Agency) put together a program (REO-to-Rental) to incentivize institutional investors to buy bulk foreclosures. Funding was provided by GSEs (Government Sponsored Entities) and from other sources. The proviso was that investors couldn't cherry-pick and had

to rent the properties for an agreed period. This was thought to be good because bulk buying allowed for economies of scale, previously not possible. Homes would thus be renovated and returned to the rental pool. Many owners became renters of their previously owned homes.

The idea of involving the private sector had its merits. Big investors were thought to be more accountable than smaller landlords due to greater transparency. They also had the capital to invest in streamlining rental management through technology. Online portals sprung up allowing for a greater range of management services such as rent collection. It also helped investors manage a diverse pool of properties. However, technological advances had a downside as they enabled large investors to identify investment properties using algorithms that scoured the property market online with specific investment criteria. Arguably, this is the point at which problems started.

While initial government programs during the 2009 crisis aimed at backstopping the downward slide in residential real estate had some success, the economy was in trouble and financial markets were struggling. For investors, the housing market looked like a good bet since values had plunged and rentals, which were in demand, now offered healthy yields in parts of the US. Institutional investors targeted their efforts where local economies and populations were growing, foreclosure activity had been high, and rental demand was strong. This inevitably led to concentrations of investments in specific locations. The sunbelt of the south and parts of the southwest became the main feeding ground. Atlanta, Jacksonville, and Charlotte, in particular, became the focus of investor activity.

The huge scale advantage of corporations meant mom-and-pop investors couldn't compete. It also meant Individual home buyers were simply priced out. Single-family homes were being vacuumed up by these large corporate entities, which often merged to give themselves even greater economies of scale and influence over market direction. In Atlanta, 25% of all purchases of single-family homes were by corporate investors. Speculation began to mount that this wholesale activity was forcing up home prices and depleting inventory. While there is little data to support this notion, there is evidence that in zip codes where investors were most active home prices appreciated markedly. Anecdotal evidence abounds of neighborhoods being overrun by high investor activity leading to widespread discontent among retail buyers.

While the need for more homes available for sale was a feature of the real estate landscape across the country, concentrated investment activity was creating its own problems. Despite earlier accounts that institutional investors were positively affecting housing by shoring up a broken housing market, it now seemed there were negative side effects resulting from their actions. Stories of mounting evictions started to spread as streamlined corporate-style management was less forgiving than smaller mom-and-pop operations. Renters were no longer so enamored with their corporate landlords. Things were starting to look ugly. Part of the problem may have been investor appetite was at odds with a recovering property market. Prices were appreciating at an alarming rate and much more so than rents. This put downward pressure on capitalization rates (yields), and made it harder to justify the investments. Perhaps institutional investors were becoming victims of their successes. If rents weren't appreciating enough then home prices had to make up the shortfall to provide a healthy total return. Concentrated feeding frenzies to snap up a shrinking pool of investments pushed up prices even further making the investments look good on paper.

Many questioned how much risk management was being applied to this seemingly reckless buying spree. Why would an investor pay so much for a property that could not be producing positive cash flows? Was there a strategy hidden from view, or were we seeing irrational exuberance in the behavior of larger investor entities? Aside from home values being pushed up, an answer to these questions may be found in how these investments were being structured. A glance back in time might help explain things.

Following the great financial crisis of 2009, it came to light that Wall Street had been active in the MBS (mortgage-backed securities) market. Mortgages with different levels of risk were repackaged into securities and sold on. The idea was higher-risk loans mixed in with quality loans would keep overall risk at tolerable levels. It was thought that as long as home values held up, the model should work. After all, home values only ever go up, which proved to be a huge error of judgment. When home prices crashed, loan defaults led to foreclosures making these mortgage securities risky bets. To make matters worse, nobody knew who was holding what. Systemic carnage followed as lenders didn't trust each other. As a result, the credit market simply dried up. Fast forward a decade or so and it appears a similar pattern has been emerging. Institutional investors have been securitizing rental incomes, as opposed to mortgages. In other words, rental investments are being repackaged and the risk sold on. The question is whether this poses a systemic risk to the housing and financial markets.

Given that institutional investors only own 3% of the rental market, it seems unlikely they pose a serious widespread risk. The securities are backed by the underlying assets, single-family home rentals, and they've been in existence since 2013 without incident. The relatively small scale of institutional investors in rentals wouldn't appear to pose widespread risk, at least to credit markets. Nonetheless, these collateralized financial instruments are exposed to interest rate risk if rates go up. They are also exposed to operations risk due to poor management, fluctuations in market rents, and home price depreciation, which weakens the collateral base. Any one of these, or in any combination, could affect the ability to pay down loans. A concern is that very little data is available on rental securitizations. With that in mind, a cautious approach to viewing them seems appropriate. It's what you don't know that can hurt you.

Foreign Buyers

Just as with institutional investors, there's been much speculation about the effects of foreign buyers on the US housing market. Foreign buyers include those who already have been residing in the US for less than two years. Again, it is difficult to say with any real certainty the extent to which foreign buyers are impacting prices, inventory, and affordability, but that they have seems likely. A paper produced by the Wharton School claims that home prices increased as a result of concentrations of foreign-born buyers purchasing homes in specific areas. However, it is doubtful that foreign buyers influence prices in the broader market simply because they comprise only 1.8% of all purchases and 2.3% of the dollar volume of all purchases in the US.

One explanation for the impact these purchases were supposedly having on prices and inventory may have been those neighborhoods were already high-growth areas. Foreign buyers may have been merely attracted by the favorable prospects. Regardless, the number of foreigners buying homes in the US has been dwindling. According to the NAR (National Association of Realtors, the number of homes sold decreased by 70% in 2023, from a peak in 2017. The reasons given for this decline were high home prices, low supply, and credit availability.

In 2023, Chinese buyers made up the biggest percentage of foreign buyers with a 13% share of homes bought by foreigners. Mexicans came in second with an 11% share, and Canada was close behind with 10%. A decade earlier, Canada had been the biggest buyer of US properties, and by a wide margin. The Chinese share has remained relatively constant over the past decade and a half starting in 2007. China has generally been the buyer of more expensive homes so has always ruled the roost in dollar terms.

Between 2014 and 2018, Chinese buyers were more active and spending more on US homes, but this trend tailed off significantly in the years that followed. The increased home-buying activity coincided with capital flight from China to avoid taxes and government scrutiny. The Chinese government had put in place capital controls in an attempt to divert money back into the flailing Chinese economy.

The median price of a home bought by a Chinese buyer in 2023, was $723,200, which is quite a big jump from previous years, which may reflect home price appreciation in the US market. Chinese bought mostly in California, Mexicans in Texas, and Canadians in Florida, with the latter state being the most popular state with foreign buyers overall. Reasons for buying help explain these regional preferences. For example, Canadians mostly buy vacation homes, usually condos. Mexicans mostly bought homes as primary residences. Chinese reasons for buying were more varied being split between vacation homes, rentals, and primary residences. About 50% of all foreign purchases are with cash with a preference for single-family homes in suburban areas of the US. Given the size of the US real estate market, it seems unlikely foreign buyers are influencing the housing market in general. On a local level, concentrations of foreign buyers may be pushing up and depleting supply.

Despite, the ebbs and flows that characterize real estate markets, the appetite for real estate remains resilient, as cash scours the globe for a place to park. Technological advances have made searches, communications, and transactions smoother. Countries where local restrictions on foreign purchases are more relaxed and where local housing markets are robust will attract foreign interest. Choices of which countries to invest in are shaped by local economies, exchange rates, immigration controls, political climates, and investment opportunities. Parts of the world that have experienced a large influx of foreign buyers have sometimes put in place measures to stem the tide. These measures usually take the form of taxes, such as stamp duty, as in the case of Singapore and Hong Kong, and a speculation and vacancy tax in Canada.

Conclusion
In conclusion, there are many aspects which help explain the affordability crisis. While a clear definition of affordability and yardstick for measuring it has eluded us, the impact the crisis has on people's lives is real and not imagined. For many, escalating housing costs

consume a large portion of incomes leaving less for basic needs creating emotional stress, and in some cases affecting health.

There are significant regional differences in affordability and its causes. The cost to build can vary according to labor and land costs. Values are also influenced by intangibles such as lifestyle and desirability leading to home prices that have become dislocated from incomes. The problem is not confined to the US. Research shows some countries may be struggling more with these kinds of housing issues, especially affordability.

Inventory is the main cause of pushing up prices, and this seems to be more as a result of homeowners not selling than not enough homes being built, although the compounding effect of years of too few homes being built has undoubtedly contributed to the problem. NIMBY-ism is a major reason given for the lack of new homes being built. Too many hoops to jump through adds to costs and timelines. The lock-in effect of higher mortgage rates disincentivizes homeowners to sell. Boomers preferring to retire in place means less inventory. With few options available to downsize and the high cost of elderly care, older homeowners have little choice but to stay put. The net result is frustration among not just among buyers and sellers, but also those working in the industry desperate to hang onto their livelihoods. The dwindling supply of homes for sale has led to dangerously high home prices, which has serious social consequences such as lost opportunities to build wealth through home equity and homelessness.

The preoccupation of many who cannot afford to buy a home is with the broken promise of the 'American Dream'. For hard-working Americans, the right to own a home is sacrosanct. For so many, then, the social contract has been breached. Fundamental to that dream is the concept of a home, which embraces security, pride, family values, memories, and financial well-being. The housing market has shown its enormous disruptive capacity when things go wrong. The lesson is things don't always go wrong on their own.

Language plays an important part in our interpretation of events. So far, we have talked about high home prices in terms of affordability, which is a euphemism for an over-valued market or even a bubble. Affordability refers to incomes being insufficient as opposed to prices being too high. While that may be the case in many instances, valuations over the last two decades point to something more serious. In the next chapter, we'll dive into the concept of value and look at valuation methods currently in use to see how they contribute to the current housing crisis.

Chapter 3

Hmm! Seems expensive for what it is.

In this chapter, the focus of attention will be on the residential real estate industry. When we speak of the industry, we refer to Realtors, trade associations, lending organizations, and related entities such as listing services, appraisers, and even the government. We will examine whether any or all of these entities contribute negatively to the real estate market. And if they have, in what ways?

In recent times, the NAR has been kept busy with lawsuits claiming it, and some of its members, have conspired to keep Realtor commissions artificially inflated. The organization boasts a huge membership and receives a vast number of small contributions that it uses to lobby government. It wields enormous power that is used to influence policy in the interests of the industry. Some argue those interests are self-serving and can create 'agency' problems commonly known as conflicts of interest.

There is evidence of information asymmetry in the housing market. This refers to the unequal access to information giving one party an unfair advantage over another. He who owns the data controls the narrative. Another major question arises over how valuations are conducted. Does a system that relies on 'comps' (comparable prices) become too easily detached from the fundamentals of value, namely, its constituent parts; labor materials, land values, and income-to-price? If so, then how do these things impact home prices and affordability?

The importance of the real estate industry to the economy means governments are prone to over-subsidize housing, exacerbating the distortions rather than offering long-term solutions. Solving problems with the housing market goes deeper than a few simple fixes such as building more homes, or lowering interest rates. By taking a deeper dive into these types of issues it is hoped conclusions can be drawn about whether these factors are detrimental and in what ways.

Housing and the Economy

The enormous size of the real estate market globally helps explain its outsized importance to economies, especially in consumer-driven developed economies. According to Savills, a leading property advisor, the value of homes globally was nearly $380 trillion in 2022, which is bigger than global equity and bond markets combined, and many times the size of global GDP. Most of that value is tied up in residential real estate. From 2019 to 2022, residential real estate outperformed both equities and bonds. China owns 26% of the total global real estate value with the US comprising 19%. Per population, however, the greater share of residential real estate value resides in the wealthiest nations and not the most populous ones.

In a report issued by the NAR in 2024, housing increasingly drives economic growth. It does this through construction, sales, and renovations, which feed through to other industries such as retail and services. It also leads to job growth and increased consumer spending. Homeowners need furniture and require contractors for a range of home-related jobs. Realtors and the mortgage industry are obvious beneficiaries of the housing sector. The report claims that each home sale in the median price range generated $125,000 in 2023, which equates to two jobs being created. It's not clear exactly how this job creation number is calculated, but it seems the NAR is looking at real estate's contribution to the economy and extrapolating job growth from it. In terms of income generated from home sales, our old friends California and Hawaii lead the way, which is unsurprising given the high home prices commanded in both states. However, the two well-heeled sisters do not steal the top spots for income expressed as a percentage of local GDP. They got to Florida, Nevada, Delaware, and Arizona. Interestingly, the NAR explains California's number one spot in the valuation charts in terms of lifestyle as well as its economy, while Hawaii's valuations are a reflection of population density. Sunshine and coastlines add a premium to prices.

Both the Savills' and NAR's reports highlight a preoccupation with positive aspects of the real estate market. The enormous growth in values is taken for granted with no hint of any potential downside such dramatic growth may portend. While it can't be expected either entity would seek to damage their own industry with negative reporting, it does go to show an industry inclined to ignore balance where it doesn't suit them. One would expect a modicum of caution in the tone of the reports, or at least an explanation for how this growth in valuation came about. The casual reader is left to believe all is well, but in reality, a housing crisis has been unfolding. And that crisis has its roots in excessive valuations. It is in this sense that the industry appears to be more preoccupied with projecting a positive narrative and less with warning of potential risks that lay ahead.

National Association of Realtors (NAR)
The NAR is the mouthpiece for the industry in the US. It is large and carries considerable influence among policymakers. Some would argue too much. This of course does not detract from all the valuable services the NAR provides to its members. Nevertheless, it has come in for some criticism. In 2023, the Wall Street Journal reported on an antitrust lawsuit against the organization and a couple of its bigger members. The lawsuit claims there has been a violation of the Sherman Antitrust Act. Essentially, this is due to the fixed 6% commission, half of which is offered to buyer brokers and is advertised on the MLS (Multiple Losing Service) website.

The MLS pools together data on the vast majority of home sales. The commission is said to be too high compared to other developed countries and creates a conflict of interest since the buyer's broker is not incentivized to act in their client's best interests. This happens because commissions are based on the selling price, so brokers are less incentivized to help buyers negotiate a better price. The NAR counters this by saying its members are required to abide by its code of ethics to prevent any conflict of interest.

There is also the question of buyers being 'steered' to homes that offer brokers higher commissions, and away from homes that offer lower commissions. This is evidenced by fewer page views of online listings and the time it takes to sell homes with lower commissions. The argument goes sellers should have a choice not to pay the buyer's commission, and buyers should be able to negotiate the commission they pay. Commissions are supposed to be 'negotiable', but that doesn't mean brokers will accept a lower commission. So, in reality, they are fixed at 6%. Attempts to break away from the MLS model to create more competition and drive down fees have met with fierce resistance from the industry. The NAR's defense against commission-rigging charges leveled at the organization is that it does not set commissions itself. It claims these are negotiated between clients and brokers. Whatever the case, it appears the lawsuit was successful and has led to changes that include removing the buyer-broker commission from the MLS.

Notwithstanding the merits of the lawsuit, there are possible downsides that follow from it. For example, buyers will now have to pay brokers for services rendered. Commissions ensured payment only resulted from a successful transaction. A fee-based system could mean extra costs for buyers, who may want to see many homes before finding one they like. There's little doubt brokers are needed for most transactions. The buying process is complex and brokers help navigate it. However, changes to remuneration could also pose a challenge to the profession, and many may have to leave the industry altogether. This would then reduce NAR membership fees and diminish its lobbying power. Many may argue in favor of that because the industry is overcrowded and wields too much influence over policymakers. In fact, there is dissent within its ranks. A large number of members surveyed said they would drop their membership if it weren't for the valuable data held on the MLS system. Access to it is fundamental to brokers. They would lose all access to it if they dropped their membership. One reason for this dissatisfaction is that the NAR has become 'bloated, arrogant, and complacent', according to one report. Does all of this have consequences for the housing market?

It's not clear that changing the way buyer-brokers are paid will have a significant impact on housing on its own. That is something that will more likely work itself out. If the evidence is credible that commissions create a conflict of interest and artificially increase home values then the lawsuits would appear to be justified.

Controlling the Narrative
A lack of public access to information creates a problem because it makes consumers vulnerable to manipulation. Unhealthy market conditions can prevail in an information vacuum. If homes are over-valued and the narrative portrays this in a positive light, it poses a risk since it dilutes checks against further volatility. Reticence surrounding potential risks stems from a belief transparency creates panic and can have negative consequences. However, opacity only continues to prolong or make worse problems with housing. A belief that controlling the narrative somehow makes the problem go away seems misguided. One explanation might be a belief the government will backstop housing if things get ugly. That of course gives rise to the notion of moral hazard. The idea is simply that if the housing market were to correct significant-

ly, wide-scale damage would result and governments would do everything they can to prevent it from happening. The situation would be similar to the housing crisis in 2006. A solution to these kinds of problems is simply to inform consumers better, and we already know how to do this.

For financial markets, unlike the housing market, there is an abundance of information about financial products and much of it is freely available. Financial news and rating services regularly provide coverage of share prices, the latest industry developments, and analyses of annual financial accounts. In fact, there is too much information often making it hard to absorb and digest. So prolific is the internet with ratios, graphs, and opinions that information has become an industry all of its own. Several rating agencies offer bond ratings to help investors decide whether the issuing company is a safe bet. Information providers such as Morningstar offer detailed information on equity and bond funds. Organizations such as the SEC (Securities and Exchange Commission) exist to regulate financial markets and to help protect investors. Yet, when it comes to the housing market, considerably bigger than financial markets, and in which many more people place their life savings, we see a conspicuous absence of the kinds of information readily available in financial markets.

The reason for the abundance of stock and bond information is that financial markets are more complex with many more different types of products displaying a much greater degree of volatility than real estate. The number of daily transactions is also very high. A home sale is an infrequent transaction, where mostly borrowed funds are exchanged for a tangible good. However, the amount of money involved in buying a home is much bigger than for a typical securities purchase. A home purchase also offers no cash flows (unless it is bought as a rental investment), and can be seized by the lender if borrowers default on mortgage payments. It therefore carries different kinds of risks.

In recent decades, home prices have become amplified by the low cost of borrowing. It is not uncommon to hear about the housing market as having 'volatility', a term usually reserved for financial markets. Volatility is when prices move significantly above or below historic averages. It is usually measured in terms of stand deviation. Historically, home prices have not displayed volatility showing more of a tendency for trend lines to continue in one direction for long periods. More recent events may help explain why volatility is appearing in home prices.

In early 2022, as prices came under pressure from rising interest rates, something happened that few had predicted. Home prices began to recover. Nobody saw it coming because interest rates were expected to put downward pressure on prices, not upward pressure. At the time there were no formalized explanations for it. It is debatable whether better-informed consumers would have prevented this anomaly because not even industry experts were expecting it. It is understandable given that in 2018, when mortgage rates went up inventory increased. The two events seemed directly connected. So, when interest rates went up significantly, the logic was inventory would respond proportionately as homeowners seized the opportunity to realize home equity gains in anticipation of falling prices due to higher mortgage rates.

Housing information is crucial to understanding where we are in the property cycle. While the NAR offers median price updates, and the Case Shiller index tracks prices based on repeat sales, little else is publicized. Moreover, most information on housing is conveyed via news stories and informally through social media or word of mouth where it is susceptible to misrepresentation. For example, when year-on-year prices are reported as increasing, it may conceal the fact that prices have been decreasing monthly. If a home valued at $500,000 increased to $575,000 over six months, but then fell back to $525,000 in the following six months this would be reported as a year-on-year price increase even though prices had fallen significantly. Context is vital in understanding direction, trends, dynamics, and the cycle.

Distortions can occur when information is conveyed informally. Homeowners tend to exaggerate what they believe their homes are worth. This not only leads to unrealistic expectations, but also denial with homeowners becoming reluctant to sell their homes, or insisting their homes are listed at unrealistic prices. Realtors will often accept instructions to list a home that is over-priced just to secure the business. The hope is that as the home sits without attracting offers, the homeowner will eventually see the light and lower the price. It's hard to imagine how this kind of behavior is in anyone's best interests. A better-informed seller is less likely to follow this route.

Housing Indicators
Aside from price information, there are other housing indicators, but these require digging deeper than the surface. They can be found on the websites of listing services such as Redfin and Zillow. Examples include the list-to-sales ratio, which indicates whether homes are selling at, above, or below asking prices. Normally, homes are listed slightly above what the seller expects to achieve. This changes when a strong sellers 'market emerges, since homes may sell above asking price.

The number of price reductions and how many days homes are sitting on the market help determine whether prices may soon be softening. The volume of sales and months supply together show how the balance from buyer to seller market may be shaping up. Slowing sales and expanding inventory put pressure on prices and indicate a buyer's market may be on the horizon. Other stress indicators are increasing default and foreclosure rates, which also works in favor of buyers.

For the more diligent, macroeconomic data is also useful in decision-making. For example, is the economy heading towards a recession? Recessions are usually considered bad times to buy a home due to uncertainty in the job market. On the other hand, downturns are usually accompanied by interest rate cuts that translate into lower borrowing costs. A slowing economy and increasing unemployment will put downward pressure on home prices as home sales slow and inventory increases.

Valuation
Probably the most controversial concept to do with real estate, especially residential real estate is valuation. This is because there is an element of subjectivity in valuing a home, especially re-sale homes. Price and value are not the same. What a buyer is willing to pay for something does not necessarily reflect the value of that thing. Most of us have an innate sense of value, or worth. Whether buying items from a grocery store or larger household items such as furniture we have an inner point of reference about whether something is expensive, or is fairly priced. How many times have we caught ourselves saying, we 'feel' the price for something is high? When we do this we are deferring to our instincts. We'd prefer to shop around before deciding.

When it comes to buying a home, all too often instincts and sense of value let us down. Our senses are bombarded by often misleading information that plays on our emotions. Quite often the information is just not available to guide us. We allow ourselves to become pressured into making decisions, sometimes wrong ones. We are led to believe value, or the price we pay is subordinate to the monthly nut. In practical terms measuring income against borrowing costs makes sense, but when borrowing costs deviate significantly from historical averages, price becomes sensitive to distortions and should not be neglected.

Cash buyers' perceptions of value will be different from borrowers'. Paying a large sum of money in cash focuses the mind much more on value, or at least it should. For some cash buyers, the innate sense of value can easily be lost, particularly in over-heated markets where competition for homes puts pressure on buyers to make quick decisions. Default risk is absent for cash purchases, but the difference between making a financially good or bad choice remains. Simply being aware of whether the asking price seems like a lot to pay for what is on offer can hold in check harmful impulses. Greater awareness of value would help curb irrational home price appreciation. If we lose sight of the importance of value, we are complicit in letting prices run away with themselves.

So, in what ways can we determine value? In the financial world, value is inextricably linked to cash flows. In real estate, the cost to build is a starting point. Affordability is what should keep prices linked to fundamentals, but it is an elastic concept and doesn't always fulfill its function. In the following paragraphs, value is examined in more detail using popular valuation techniques. Their shortcomings will also be looked at in terms of consequences for the housing market.

In residential real estate, the most common method for valuing a property is to use comparable prices, or 'comps', as they are more commonly called. This involves making comparisons with similar homes that sold recently in nearby locations to arrive at an asking price. Adjustments are then made based on things like square footage, curb appeal, condition, and so on. The simplicity of the method avoids all sorts of unnecessary and time-consuming calculations so shortens transaction times. Where the method fails is when home prices have become detached from the fundamentals. The method doesn't measure whether homes being compared to are themselves 'fairly' valued. It may be these comps already deviate significantly from historical averages. This has been very apparent following the 2006 housing crisis.

Apart from the practical aspects of the comps method of valuation, other reasons help explain its popular use. One of those is found in the concept of 'fair market value', defined as the willingness of a buyer to pay a predetermined price to a seller. Unlike new homes that have costs built into their prices, resale homes deteriorate with age, so a natural inclination would be to depreciate their values. However, a home's utility is not considered diminished since homes are built to last for years, and well beyond the average ownership period. So value assumes a subjective element irrespective of age. Homes that do show signs of serious deterioration are priced accordingly and may reflect some or all of the costs involved in restoring a home to good condition. But this will be decided during negotiations and won't necessarily be formally costed. Equally, new home prices may reflect market prices and not just costs and margins. Subjective added-value is zero-sum.

The main criticism of the comps method is it has no inbuilt mechanism for sounding alarms bells should prices escalate at a much faster pace than incomes, inflation, or rents. This is because value is derived almost entirely from sold prices, and not fundamentals. Neither does it take into account the kinds of irrational behavior we see when competition to buy homes heats up. It is much better suited to a market where supply and demand are in balance, and no distortions have occurred as a result of extended periods of low interest rates. Its usefulness in determining true value is limited, therefore, being based on the assumption comps are efficiently priced. In this sense, it not only fails to inhibit conditions under which home prices escalate to unsustainable high levels, it may actually encourage over-valuations.

The lack of a rigorous valuation method applied to residential real estate is to some degree instrumental in allowing home prices to drift, sometimes appreciably. The widely used comps method is only a relative measure of value so depends on efficient price discovery. However, this doesn't explain why prices become and remain unsustainable or unaffordable. Lenders have strict criteria and use appraisers to value homes before lending. This should act as a check on volatile prices, but it doesn't always seem to. When the cost to borrow remains low for an extended period prices become artificially inflated. Lenders are then faced with either cutting back lending, which hurts business, or loosening lending criteria. Allowing prices to fall is not in lenders' interests because it increases default risk, which impacts their balance sheets negatively. Looser lending criteria also amplify default risk. So, what would solve this problem? Are there other methods that could and should be used to determine value? It seems one is needed when conditions are ripe for their unchecked appreciation.

Fundamental Valuation
There are two other commonly used methods to value real estate. The DCF (discounted cash flow) method, and the replacement cost method. The DCF (discounted cash flow) method is not often used to value residential real estate. It is more suited to commercial real estate, equities, and business projects, which are all investments that are expected to produce income streams. The idea is simply that income can be used to determine the value of an asset. The way this is normally explained is that future income flows are discounted using a discount rate to produce a present value. The discount rate can be a required rate of return—what an investor expects or wants—or, it can be the return of an alternative investment. Those (discounted) cash flows are then added up to arrive at a value. A common criticism of DCF is that it is only as good as the assumptions built into it, such as the discount rate and expected future cash flows. For residential real estate, projected cash flows would be an assumed net rental income based on rental comps. The discount rate could be a required rate of return, for example, 5%, or the risk-free rate of a ten-year government bond. The computa-

tion is complex and requires a spreadsheet with several inputs and other formulas such as the CAPM (capital assets pricing model), which itself has built-in assumptions.

Although DCF is not a perfect science, it does offer a more scientific approach compared to using the comps method. Another obvious criticism of using the DCF model for real estate is it doesn't take into account the unique features of a home. On the positive side, using rents is a step closer to a fundamentals-based valuation. Rents have always been considered a useful yardstick for what someone can afford. This is because landlords are careful to ensure tenants' incomes are adequate to meet rent demands comfortably. In addition, landlords only charge what the rental market can bear to ensure minimum vacancies, a direct cost affecting cash flows. Rents are also subject to other forces such as supply and demand, and all things being equal, they keep affordability in check. However, as with home prices, this isn't always the case. What should happen and reality are often two different things.

In 2021 and 2022, rent growth exploded only to drop dramatically in 2023, but remained above pre-pandemic levels. In 2022, over 12 million homes were spending more than 50% of their income on rent. When rents become so distorted that tenants are forced to pay more than they can afford, the DCF model can lead to distortions in valuations. This is because cash flows use rental comps and are projected into the future. Although the outsized rent growth in the above instance was short-lived and the circumstances unusual, it goes to show rents can be quite volatile and, therefore, not always a stable measure of what renters can afford.

Despite the shortcomings of the DCF model for valuation purposes it nevertheless provides a better guide to intrinsic values than using comps alone. There is a hybrid DCF model called the Gordon Growth Model. Its attraction is its simplicity. When used for valuing stocks it uses dividend growth to calculate value. In theory, net operating income of a rental property can be substituted for dividends. However, it is rare to hear this method being used in a residential real estate context.

The third model of valuation uses the cost to replace a home. This is essentially how much it would cost to rebuild a home with the same specifications, using current costs for material and labor. It is similar to what an insurer might pay out if a home was a total loss. Basing a home's value on readily identifiable tangibles offers a useful valuation measure. However, land values fluctuate and are determined by use. Disaggregating constituent parts of a home's value would be useful. However, it seems unlikely such a breakdown would be widely adopted.

Out of all three valuation methods, the comps method is the most used for residential property, but as mentioned already, it has serious drawbacks in over-heated markets. Valuation methods that aim to calculate intrinsic worth also have their limitations but could provide an alternative where comps are unreliable. Using a combination of methods might help in identifying value discrepancies where results diverge significantly. In financial modeling, a system called the 'football field' is used to do just this. Value is calculated by using weighted averages of different valuation models. The idea is appealing but time-consuming so may not be practical for the vast majority of residential real estate transactions. They are more suited to commercial real estate that has its own set of tools. Could some of these be applied to residential real estate?

Commercial real estate applies rigorous tests to determine value. Essentially, investors of commercial property are looking for a return, so will estimate cash flows against the price of a property to decide whether or not to invest in it. If the price is too high, or rents too low it will impact returns negatively. One method for determining this is the GRM (Gross Rent Multiplier) ratio. It is calculated by dividing market price by the annual rent. For example, if a home is valued at $120,000 and produces an annual gross rent of $10,000, the GRM is $120,000 / $10,000 = 12. Having calculated the GRM, it can then be used to establish other property values, simply by multiplying the ratio by the gross rent. A worked example is as follows:

Gross annual rent x GRM = Home Value

$8,000 x 12 = $96,000

Another ratio commonly used by investors to determine whether an investment is acceptable is to divide forecasted NOI (net operating income) by the capitalization rate, or 'cap rate'. The cap rate acts as a required rate of return and represents the ratio of net return to price. It is a commonly used calculation to determine an investment feasibility. Dividing NOI by the cap rate results in a value, or price to pay for a property. For example, taking an NOI of $252m and a cap rate of 5%, the calculation is as follows:

$$NOI \div Cap\ Rate = Property\ Price$$

$$\$252m \div 5\% = \$5,040m$$

It is important to note that, as with the DCF model, assumptions are made about future rental income and costs. Using past data gives a more reliable measure of a current value, but past data is not necessarily a reliable indication of the future. The question is whether commercial real estate valuation models can be applied to residential real estate. For this to work estimates would need to be made of rents and costs using comparable homes. Accuracy improves when unique aspects of a residential home, such as curb appeal, condition, etc are captured in the numbers.

So, why don't appraisers of residential real estate use any of these intrinsic value methods? A simple answer may be tradition, but also these more mechanical methods don't allow for price elasticity. In other words, they may restrict the ability to negotiate in a competitive environment. In a buyer's market, the buyer can negotiate a price below the list price. Likewise, when sellers have the upper hand, competition from buyers can push the price above the list price. The comps method of valuation is more forgiving where prices fluctuate. It is also more suited to a commission-based transaction model. A criticism of this might be that it necessarily leads to price manipulation and volatility since higher prices mean higher commissions.

New Technology
Although it seems very small advances are being made in the field of valuation, new technologies are making some inroads. Automated Valuation Models (AVMs) have been around for some time but now have enhanced capabilities due to AI (artificial intelligence). AVMs are computer systems that use algorithms to calculate property values drawing on the vast pool of data collected on transactions. As such, they are invaluable to appraisers, especially where a large number of homes need to be valued. Advantages of using these types of models are they allow for greater efficiency and cost-effectiveness. Many online listing services use them such as Zillow. Price is the main input, which is then adjusted for variables such square footage, number of bedrooms, etc. Since the models are computer-based, they can't adjust for subjective variables such as curb appeal or the condition of the property, so they are often used in conjunction with appraisers who help fill this gap.

One downfall of AVMs is they rely on comps data to value properties. In this sense, they don't offer an advantage over the method used by most appraisers. The valuation is, therefore, merely based on similar sales and doesn't take into account the intrinsic value of a property. They won't tell you whether a home is over-valued or under-valued, just that it is similarly valued. There is no reason why algorithms can't be adapted to calculate intrinsic value that could then be displayed alongside the list, or market price, so people can make a better judgment about buying and selling. After all, the comparison between a stock's intrinsic value and its market price is available on many financial websites such as Morningstar and investing platforms.

Valuation Examples
The importance of valuation cannot be over-emphasized. The current system of relying on comps is vulnerable to exploitation and price momentum detached from economic reality. It is also susceptible to 'anchoring bias', a behavior linked to an over-dependence on prima facie information. Comps are used because they offer a quick and simple method relying on one metric combined with subjective judgment. Intrinsic valuation models, such as DCF, are cumbersome and have too many in-built assumptions to be practical in every situation. The advantage of them, however, is they use a mathematical approach to remove some of the subjectivity in home valuation. The following paragraph analyses the value of an actual home in California using the various valuation techniques discussed above. The exercise will then compare the results of the valuation models.

The property is based in Los Angeles County and a market price was calculated using the average estimated price of three online listing services, Zillow, Redfin, and Realtor. This was done because there was some variation in the price estimates between the listing services. This again highlights the difficulties with valuation. Zillow's estimates for rental income were used because the actual rent seemed a little low compared to recent rental comps. It should be remembered that rents at the time were considered high. For the DCF calculation, a 2% growth rate was used for both future rents and home price appreciation. The period used was 15 years, which is more or less the average time a home is owned. The GRM was generated automatically by an online source that claims to use historical data generated by commercial real estate investors. Expenses have similarly been estimated.

Market price of home = $663,596

Valuation Method 1
NOI ÷ Cap Rate = Value
$23,313 ÷ 3.86% = $603,964

Valuation Method 2
Gross Rent x GRM = Value
$40,788 x 14.15 = $577,150

Valuation Method 3
DCF (disc rate 5%) = Present Value (PV)
Present Value = $630,874

All three methods produce a value below the average of the three online listing services. In the case of the GRM method, it was somewhat lower. This may be because the multiplier was determined by investors' required rate of return. A criticism of these forms of valuations is the accuracy of the assumptions. For example, the DCF model uses rental and home price comps, which themselves may already be inflated. In this instance, the rent comps were certainly inflated since the actual rent was somewhat lower. It also makes assumptions about the future value of money. The two other methods compare price to rent to determine investment criteria. Assuming all investors will only be seeking investments that offer good returns valuations are going to be closer to intrinsic value. However, since rents can display volatility there is no guarantee of healthy returns unless a cushion has been built into the model to allow for variables.

All three valuations came in lower than the comps, and the margins between them were not huge. Given the relatively minor differences, it would be tempting to conclude a certain level of accuracy. However, that would be misleading because all three methods use similar kinds of metrics. And they all derive their results, to one degree or another, from relative measures. Nevertheless, if we take an average of the results, it comes in 9% lower than the comps, which is not an insignificant saving from a buyer's perspective.

There is one more variable that may offer useful insight in our search for intrinsic value and that is income. The level of income to debt payment shows how much buyers can afford. For this exercise, I've enlisted the help of AI and have used affordability data* produced by the CAR (California Association of Realtors) as the basis for the calculations. California is a useful lab rat because it suffers from a huge affordability crisis. According to the CAR, only 17% of Californians could afford the median price of $900,720 in the first quarter of 2024. These numbers are very concerning in their implications for the housing market.

*These data and accompanying graphs can be found in the CAR publication, 'California Housing Affordability Update for the first quarter of 2024'

The affordability problem is not a new phenomenon. And it did not come about because of COVID-19. It has been in the making since 2012, first reaching a peak in 2007. Of course, the problem has not been restricted to California. In 2012, 71% of Americans could afford a median-priced home. In 2024, that percentage dropped to 37%. The amount of income required to service a loan in California has increased 270% for the same period. Increased mortgage rates are a big part of that story, but home prices have played an equally big role. Instead of prices going down when mortgage rates increased, they went up adding to the affordability woes.

It's worth mentioning that not all of California suffers from this dilemma. The county of Lassen for example, meets the affordability benchmark with over 50% of people being able to afford the median price implying a balanced market. According to Redfin, the median price in Lassen County was $245,000 in July 2024, which is nearly half the median price nationally. At the other end of the spectrum, the county of Mono also in California gives a more severe affordability reading than the state as a whole. The adage real estate is local lives on.

A couple of words of caution are warranted before starting the income calculation. The CAR affordability index is based on median prices and median incomes. Firstly, median prices vary from source to source. Online listing services such as Zillow and Redfin have somewhat lower estimations than the CAR. The more important thing to bear in mind is median incomes and median prices are not a perfect match, because many people cannot afford to buy any home. In inner cities, it's not unusual to find 50% of dwellers are renters. Many people are simply not in a position to buy, because they lack the income to buy even the lowest-priced homes. One suggestion is to remove this lower income strata from the data pool. This will have the effect of pushing up the medium income and may offer a more realistic match than the median income. The AI calculations below do not take this into account, since it would have added a layer of complexity.

> *To determine by what percentage of homes are over-valued and what the median home price should be for affordability, we need to establish a relationship between the current*

affordability (17%) and the desired affordability (50%).

Current Affordability: Median Price is $900,720, affordable to 17% of Californians. Desired Affordability: Affordable to 50% of Californians. Median Price is unknown (X)

Understanding Affordability: The median home price is considered affordable when 50% of the population can purchase it. Currently, only 17% can afford it at $900,720.

We need to determine the percentage by which the current median price is higher than the price that would be affordable to 50% of the population.

Calculation
Affordability Factor: The current price ($900,720) is affordable to 17%, but we want it to be affordable to 50%.

Assume affordability is directly proportional to the price, so:

$$17 \div 50 = X \div \$900{,}720$$

Solve for X:

$$X = \$900{,}720 \times 17 \div 50$$

$$X = \$900{,}720 \times 0.34$$

$$= \$306{,}244$$

Although the above AI income calculations do not use the same home used in the previous valuations, it is clear something is very amiss. How is it possible that the median price is 2.94 times the price that people should be paying based on affordability criteria? One problem is with inconsistent data. The range of median incomes available from different sources is significant. There are also quite large differences quoted in the median price of homes between online information services. Mixing data between sources could also compound inconsistencies and distort measurements. In defense of the results, it's worth remembering the CAR provides data that makes a compelling case that California has a serious affordability problem. The median price in Lassen County further supports the view that the median price for California should be much lower.

In conclusion, we are left with a significant gulf in valuation results between comps, intrinsic values, and the affordability measure. Refining the various methods and data used may go some way to improving the results. So, the question remains whether current valuation methods, or lack thereof, contribute in some way to distorting home values and in so doing exacerbate the affordability crisis. For the most part, it seems they do. It is pretty clear from sifting through online listing sources that home prices in many locations are high, even extreme. Home price indices support the view that prices are high. It is possible the upward trend could continue if mortgage rates decrease and demand continues to exceed supply. How long that can continue is anyone's guess. A popular definition of a bubble is you don't know you are in one until it bursts. That is an unfortunate way of viewing things since it is reactive rather than proactive in preventing potential risks.

A proactive approach would be to inform buyers and sellers better about valuations. Indicating even a range of possible values based on mathematical models would be helpful. Just as with financial securities, a fair market valuation could be published alongside the listing price giving buyers a broader idea about a home's value. If the list price of a home is well above the fair market value, a buyer then has an option either to negotiate a better price or seek homes where values offer better opportunities for building home equity and avoiding burdensome costs. Consumers should be encouraged to nurture their instincts for what feels like good value and what doesn't. Questioning whether something is good value is the first step before committing to buying. If it doesn't seem like it's worth it, then probably it isn't.

Chapter 4

Of course it's safe, everyone's doing it.

This chapter starts with a fun quiz. There is no right or wrong answer because it all depends on your personality. The questions are constructed to determine your behavioral responses to typical situations involving investing and by association buying a home.

Answer with a simple "yes" or "no", and don't ponder too long on the answers.

Quiz

If a lot of people are doing something you would like to do, does that make it more likely you'll do it? Yes/No

If you think home prices are increasing and you find two articles, one which states prices are falling, and one which states they are increasing, would you read the latter article first? Yes/No

If your home increased in value do you think it is because you made a wise decision? Yes/No

Do you think home prices only go up, and that buying a home is risk-free? Yes/No

If your home was decreasing in value and you wanted to sell, would you wait to see if it picked up in value? Yes/No

Do you think homeowners tend to over-value their homes? Yes/No

When you first see a home listed at a certain price, do you believe the information must be correct and reflect fair market value? Yes/No

If home prices were going up while you were looking for a home, would this make you more likely to buy than wait? Yes/No

Does losing money worry you more than gaining money makes you happy? Yes/No

If you tossed a coin nine times and each time it came up 'tails', is it more likely the next toss will also be tails? Yes/No

If home prices increased each month for a year, do you think it is inevitable they will continue to do so? Yes/No

If home prices were falling and you wanted to sell, would you hold out for the price you wanted because you believed your home was worth that price? Yes/No

If home prices increased year-on-year, do you think home prices are still going up? Yes/No

If you answered "yes" to most of the questions read on. That is not because you gave the wrong answers. The idea is just to draw your attention to certain behavioral symptoms you might not be aware you have.

In previous chapters, we looked at how the real estate industry, monetary policy, valuation methods, regulations, and government incentives have helped shape the housing market. There is another major factor that plays an important role in housing market dynamics and that is us, the consumer. More specifically, it is our behavior that is responsible for so much that happens, and so much that can go wrong in housing. In the world of finance, behavior has been the subject of considerable research. It has become a major discipline in helping explain why we act in certain ways under certain conditions. When markets are going through periods of turmoil it often leads to the kinds of behavior that can work against us to the point of recklessness. It seems we can't help ourselves, because we are often incapable of holding our emotions in check. It might be said our behavior makes risky environments worse by acting in ways that are irrational and impulsive. Warren Buffet put it best when we said successful investing is more about temperament than intellect. You are less likely to make mistakes if you take a more circumspect and calm.

While a lot of research has been conducted into behavioral finance, not much has been conducted in the area of real estate. This seems odd given the size and importance of the industry. Since the housing market shares a lot in common with financial markets, behavioral finance concepts can be used as a framework for analyzing the buying and selling of homes. We start with the idea consumers are fickle and biased and that consumerism drives our economies. Advertising manipulates our cravings to help us part with our cash. This happens despite some purchases having little to no utility. Yet we seem happy to participate in the deception as a trade-off to get our 'fix'. When it comes to investments and homes, however, more is at stake as larger sums are normally changing hands.

Behavioral finance revolves around the idea we suffer from many biases. It is used to explain the many ways in which we are inclined to behave in this or that way given certain kinds of circumstances. In everyday use, bias refers to an inclination towards a particular, often narrow, frame of referencing, or one-sidedness. It often has emotional connotations, which can work against our own best interests. An example of this behavior is when we display what is termed 'confirmation bias'. This is when we seek out information that confirms what we already believe to be true. This reinforces our belief in something. It confirms our bias and blocks out other information that counters this belief.

Confirmation Bias
Good examples of confirmation bias show up when we do internet searches. We will use words like "home prices increase". Because of how search engines work, we are more likely to get results showing that home prices are increasing. While it may be true national home prices are increasing, regionally things could be very different. Search engine algorithms aren't critical-thinking machines. They simply use words to find relevant information and will keep sending us similar information. They are configured to reinforce bias. The more entrenched we are in our bias, the more likely we are to ignore opposing views. To guard against this confirmation bias, we need to step outside our emotional enclosures and ask the opposite of what we believe to be true. We need to play the devil's advocate.

Buying a home will be the biggest financial commitment that most people will ever make. It should therefore be given consideration commensurate with its size. However, all too often we become distracted from the task. The brain is flooded with many of the emotions behaviorists try to warn us about. This may be due to a lack of information, inexperience, or simply being overwhelmed by everything from contracts, financial considerations, what friends and family are advising, and what our professional advisors are telling us. To cope with all the information and emotions, we apply cognitive biases that offer shortcuts to arrive at decisions.

Interestingly, many of those we rely on for quality information may also be subject to the same behavioral biases as us. This should give us serious pause for thought. For instance, your lender may be putting too much faith in the home appraisal. Your Realtor may be 'anchoring' your offer tightly to comps (comparable prices), despite clear signals homes may be over-valued. This anchoring bias even affects appraisers who will often use pre-existing information, such are the previous price sold to determine value. The result can create an upwardly spiraling momentum, where prices are simply chased higher and higher. Demand and supply no longer hold them in check, and price discovery takes on a life of its own.

The idea that markets are efficient and self-correcting becomes less convincing as a theory when prices become detached from their foundations. Any notion that somehow things will work themselves out needs to be quickly dispelled. Our behavior is part of the story that explains why this happens. We are unwittingly helping create the conditions for home values to spiral out of control. Our behavior becomes self-fulfilling and self-reinforcing making matters worse.

Anchoring Bias

When a home is first listed, the price it is given acts as an 'anchor' for how buyers, Realtors, sellers, and even appraisers perceive its value. We have an anchoring bias towards the first piece of information we see, believing it to be correct. This tips negotiations in favor of the seller who has more leverage in negotiations, and makes it difficult for the buyer to challenge it in any meaningful way. The exception to this rule is when it is a buyer's market.

Anchoring heuristics is the process of using readily available information such as current list price, or even prior prices. Heuristics in housing is price discovery by trial and error. It seeks to find solutions to questions quickly rather than wading through a lot of information. This is how we generally navigate our daily lives. This cognitive process is more suited to easy and repetitive tasks where outcomes are more predictable. When it comes to more complex tasks that require slow and methodical thinking, the heuristic behavior is prone to error, which can affect outcomes. When it comes to the housing market, anchoring heuristics is thought to contribute not just to mispricing, but ultimately to speculative asset bubbles. In practical terms, offers to buy a home will generally be in line with the list price. Since online listing services draw their information from a central source they will all present the same information, which reinforces the legitimacy of prices based on comps.

Anchoring bias also explains why out-of-state buyers find themselves at a disadvantage and tend to overpay for homes. They place too much validity on the first information they see, and may not have access to other more local information. For example, there may be external factors that only someone living locally would be privy to, and which might affect the value of a home. However, it is likely an out-of-state buyer would be using a local Realtor who would have local knowledge. Also, a lot of information is available online, which everyone has access to, regardless of where they live. Possible other untoward considerations may simply come to light during the due diligence process.

One of the more concerning and perplexing aspects of this anchoring behavior is that it infects everyone from buyers and sellers to Realtors and appraisers. A buyer's broker is supposed to be acting in the best interests of their client. They should be negotiating the best price for them, but are driven by commissions. The higher the selling price, the higher the commission. The previous chapter describes the lawsuit aimed at the industry for its part in commission rigging. A home appraiser is the final arbiter of price. His or her role is to determine the value of the home, and whether the negotiated price is reflective of the various value aspects of the home within the context of the housing market. It should be an independent, unbiased, and objective view. Yet there is evidence that even appraisers are not immune from the effects of anchoring bias. They will base their evaluation on many factors, but one of those will be comps prices.

It is unlikely they will value a home that deviates significantly from the comps. Other evidence also points to a tendency of appraisers to over-value properties if previously they had been criticized for under-valuing properties.

Herding

The most common behavioral trait is 'herding'. We tend to behave as a herd because we rationalize that if many people are doing something they must be right. We intuitively feel there must be a collective wisdom in the crowd. This thought process fails to consider the paradox that each individual in the herd is acting on that same impulse. It is a cognitive error and conjures up the image of a herd of sheep running towards a cliff edge blind to the risk of plunging to the depths below. An example of this herding behavior might be the decision to buy a home. You want to buy a home but may have some reservations. Yet, so many people are racing towards doing the same, you rationalize they must know something you don't.

Herding behavior impacts decisions—often negatively—more than any other behavior. As with anchoring, herding contributes to price momentum, which can lead to asset bubble formations. This kind of behavior is what Alan Greenspan, a Former Federal Reserve Bank Chairman referred to as 'irrational exuberance'. The term was later adopted by Professor Shiller to describe how people behaved during the 2006 housing crisis. The herd pushes up prices, which attracts more investment as the price is bid ever upwards. The behavior is observable in financial markets and is exploited by traders using technical analysis to try and predict the price direction of equities.

As markets become more volatile we see more herding. In the lead-up to the 2006 housing bubble, herding behavior was very apparent. Bidding wars became voracious and commonplace, pushing up prices until they were no longer sustainable. In 2022, a similar behavior was observed. Buyers became frenetic seemingly unaware they were getting caught up in the irrational exuberance. Herd behavior unquestionably contributed to the 2006 and 2022 bubbles in home prices. The same behavior was very apparent in financial markets during the dot-com bubble in the year 2000. One reason we fail to recognize the symptoms of these events and the behavior that leads up to them is we are vulnerable to self-deception.

Over-Confidence
We've all heard someone boasting about the value of their home, seemingly taking the credit for making a savvy buying decision. However, behaviorists warn us self-deception lurks in the shadows of our minds. The brain works on many different levels and sometimes doesn't appear to be working in our own best interests. We deceive ourselves in subtle ways that don't seem detrimental to us, but which can materially affect our lives in different ways. Not recognizing cognitive errors can lead to losses. In the financial world, it is not uncommon to find investors behaving with over-confidence, the grandest of all self-deception. Self-confidence increases as a result of successful

trades and becomes self-reinforcing. Those successes may be explained by events unrelated to skills, but the investors deceive him/herself into believing they are down to their ability and investing skills. That over-confidence often leads to over-trading, taking on more risk, and ultimately incurring losses.

Self-Attribution
Homes aren't traded on an exchange but the same self-belief can manifest itself in the same way. Homeowners often deceive themselves into thinking they bought 'well' because their home's value has increased. This is known as 'self-attribution', where we attribute successes to our skills and failures to factors we believe are beyond our control, such as simple bad luck. Homes may have risen for any number of reasons such as gentrification, a demand-supply imbalance, or low mortgage rates, which may have nothing to do with an individual's decision to buy. Self-attribution may encourage homeowners to invest in other properties taking on too much debt, so exposing themselves to unnecessary risk and financial losses. Our self-deception, over-confidence, and misplaced self-belief can blind us to broader factors that may negatively impact us. While buying a home is not the same as trading stocks, home prices may have risen in the broader market due to many factors unrelated to individual decisions to buy. While attributing successes to oneself is not a crime, it can lead to loss-making behavior.

Over-Optimism

Over-optimism is another form of self-deception. The tendency is to overestimate positive outcomes and underestimate negative ones. We believe more information necessarily leads to better outcomes, and that we, therefore, have some control over events. This skews our forecasts towards being over-optimistic. Over-optimism may manifest itself in the belief that home prices only ever go up, so the risks associated with the housing market tend to be downplayed. There is also a tendency to be both over-optimistic about interest rates, and not to react appropriately when rates change. For instance, homeowners often anticipate being able to refinance when rates lower, simultaneously trusting that their homes will increase in value. This can lead to taking on too much debt, which increases default risk when home prices don't increase, as happens. During the credit crisis in 2009, a leading cause of foreclosures was negative equity. This occurs when home prices fall below the price paid. Borrowers are then faced with paying down a loan that is greater than the new, lower value of their home.

The media is a prime source of over-optimism. News reports are narrow in their message, often reporting positive aspects and neglecting downside risks. For example, home prices may be reported as continuing to climb, but reports fail to mention valuations are seem very out of kilter with the fundamentals. We also tend to limit our judgments to only what we recall. For example, it is not uncommon for people to claim home prices only ever go up, despite the fact home prices do indeed fall. In 2012, the trough of the 2006 housing crisis, home prices had fallen by as much as 60% in some cities, yet many overlooked this past event.

To sum up, behavioral biases can interfere with the normal, rational processing of information and decision-making. Emotions play a big part in shaping the housing market. While it is easy to conclude a failing housing market has its roots in the many shortcomings of valuation techniques, monetary and fiscal policies, the regulatory environment, ZIMBY-ism, and supply issues, our behavior is equally culpable. We allow our emotions to guide our decisions. Self-deception, such as over-confidence, the illusion of knowledge, and over-optimism shape our actions. We attributable successes to ourselves, and failures to anything but ourselves. We don't adjust appropriately to new information. We actively seek out confirmation of our beliefs to justify our convictions. In so doing, we expose ourselves to avoidable risk and material loss. We suffer from the 'endowment effect', a belief our homes are more valuable than they are. We see trend lines and patterns which may be just random data. We don't understand probability, and believe the past is a good predictor of the future. We seek short, easy, and quick answers to complex problems and place too much emphasis on more recent news. We show bias towards the familiar, or the 'status quo', and resist change, preferring to stay within an environment where we feel most comfortable. For example, boomers prefer to retire in place, so their homes remain off-market, which contributes to a decrease in the supply of homes for sale. The most visible and damaging of behaviors is herding, yet we remain largely oblivious to its omnipresence. When the housing market becomes as volatile as it has in recent decades, it's largely because we allow it to do so.

Conclusion
To conclude this chapter, it is important to realize these behaviors are not easily measurable in terms of how they shape the housing market. It is not possible to claim a percentage by which behaviors increase or decrease home values, for example. That they contribute to price instability and even bubbles is not in dispute. Price momentum, volatility, and herd behavior interact with each other in this very visible way. If it were possible to arrive at an accurate fundamental value for a home, any additional value would almost certainly be attributable to one or more behavioral biases and cognitive errors. By the same token, should fundamental value be calculable, such behaviors would be less likely to occur.

There is a symbiosis between behavior and valuation discrepancies. Where price and fundamental value (as far as we can discern it) appear to diverge significantly, such as in California, behavior will have played a significant role in driving up prices. The same will also be true if prices correct. This is especially true in financial markets, where investors try to mitigate losses by selling, hedging, applying stop losses, etc. Since housing is less liquid due to long transaction times, loss aversion may manifest itself in denial and a refusal to sell at a lower price.

While emotions are hard to control, part of the blame for why we behave the way we do may be partly explained by external considerations. Readily available information on the housing market is scarce, giving rise to the notion of information asymmetry. The narrative is controlled by the industry that owns the data. As our decisions are largely uninformed, we rely on emotions, intuition, and guesswork to help guide us. It is no wonder, therefore, that we become so easily caught up in the traps our minds set for us.

Creating an awareness that checks our behavior will at least go someway to preventing these adverse behavioral traits, and in so doing, it will help us to make better decisions. The most important behaviors to be aware of are herding, confirmation bias, over-confidence, and loss aversion. Do we blindly follow the crowd? Do we only seek information that confirms our beliefs? Do we take credit where it may not be due, and do we make the wrong decisions out of an aversion towards losses?

Chapter 5

I'm from the government and I'm here to help.

Government Intervention

In previous chapters, we have examined the machinations of the housing market and how its many components, including our behavior, combine and interact to fashion the ebb and flow, and dynamics of supply and prices. Another important component to all this is the role of governments and the ramifications policy has for housing. A quick review of the history of the government's role in housing in the US reveals a gradual transition from a large federal presence to more state and local government roles. Over the years various governmental and quasi-governmental institutions have emerged to carry out policies targeting inadequacies in housing.

There's no doubt government intentions are nearly always well-meaning, especially when aimed at relieving poor living conditions, insufficient housing, and affordability. It's also laudable to expand homeownership to a wider pool of the population, so more people can benefit from building wealth and security. The question is whether governments more generally improve things or make them worse. A clue to that lies in their motives.

Governments are not driven by profits or meeting shareholders' expectations but by votes secured with policy promises. Governments perform a balancing act between promises made to voters, their ability to deliver on those promises, and competing interests within the economy and the political arena. While it's nice to believe housing policies are a force for good, there are times when the reverse seems true. And this can manifest itself in different areas of the housing market such as home prices, demand and supply, homeownership rates, wealth distributions, and even the economy itself. It would be difficult quantitatively to measure the impact of poor policies on the housing market, but history shows an undulating landscape of successes and failures. In the following paragraphs, we'll look at areas where government policy, at both the federal and state levels, has contributed to housing woes.

The mortgage market has long been the backbone of the home-ownership. It might seem unimaginable to us now, but before the Great Depression (1929-1939), mortgages were for three to five years and payments were made annually. Mortgages only covered about half the value of a home, leaving the other half somewhat exposed to a less developed lending environment. This ultimately led to a lot of foreclosures in the 1930's.

The federal government encouraged lenders to get involved in building homes and also created construction jobs. It was at this time that the creation of a governmental housing body, the Federal Housing Authority (FHA), ushered in an era of direct federal government intervention in housing to address serious housing inadequacies and support against financial losses. The FHA insured losses on loans and the buying and selling of mortgages, which were now for 20 years. The loan payment insurance eventually gave way to down payments, which was the precursor to modern-day mortgages.

The government even began building units to rent to ease the plight of so many, especially the poor, in the wake of the Great Depression. States then took over this role steered by what is now the Housing and Urban Development (HUD) department. The goal was to improve the appalling conditions that so many lived under. Many dwellings were unsanitary and unsafe, with decent housing being in short supply. Fast forward to post-WWII, and it was clear to politicians something major had to change. The answer was found in huge public housing programs. Efforts were aimed at low and even moderate incomes and involved the private sector using low-interest loans to provide affordable rental accommodation.

Public Housing

In the 1960's, the HUD introduced rent caps and refunded the difference to developers. It also subsidized loans to developers, which were then extended to individual borrowers. These subsidies reduced interest payments to a meager 1%. Public housing flourished as a result of this public-private partnership. However, not all was well on the Western front. Discrimination at all levels was rife in the allocation of public housing and lending insurance. The Fair Housing Act of 1968, was to do away with all this unfairness. By the 1970s, the business of building homes for rent met with its demise. President Nixon thought public housing was both costly and of poor quality, so he introduced rental subsidies in their place. This saw a shift away from the government's involvement in construction to providing major rental assistance. The Section 8 rental program was born. Landlords received rent subsidies in return for renting to the poorest in the community. The mixed fortunes of these programs together with other policy priorities, such as funding for the Cold War, meant government coffers were no longer in plentiful supply. Having lost their subsidies, landlords resorted to market rents to make up the difference.

By 1990, the federal government ceded control to individual states, believing things could be more effectively managed at the local level. It made sense, but what followed was a gradual decline in public housing that had simultaneously garnered a bad reputation for crime and violence. Moreover, building restrictions made it much harder for new units to be built. In consequence, the federal government's reduced role in housing seems to have given rise, at least in some measure, to the issue of affordability. Many subsidized rentals were no longer available to low-income households. As mentioned, landlords were no longer required to maintain rents at affordable levels. It also became harder for developers to raise funds to build. Priorly, they had received funding from the federal government, but now they had to seek funding from a variety of different sources making the task that much more arduous.

Crisis in the Making
In the early 2000s, mortgage lending had gotten out of hand. Home prices had formed into an enormous asset bubble, which burst creating an equally severe credit crisis leading to the Great Recession. So, in a few decades, the housing market had gone through a major transformation beginning and ending with severe economic turmoil. Government responses to the crises went from highly centralized and subsidized to transferring control to individual states and involving the private sector. Funding priorities had changed, yet intervention was not entirely absent.

The effects of the Great Recession were so damaging a whole host of reforms came into being. First and foremost, the bleeding had to stop. Programs were put in place to stem the flow of foreclosures. In 2009, President Obama introduced a huge stimulus bill. In 2010, the Dodd-Frank Act aimed at remedying the wrongs of shoddy lending practices that many believed were at the core of the crisis. Lenders were to become better capitalized to weather possible future financial storms, and lending criteria became tighter to protect borrowers from becoming over-burdened with debt.

Perhaps most controversially, tax credits were introduced in 2008 at both the federal and state levels aimed at stimulating housing demand, especially among first-time buyers. This was controversial because tax-payer money was being used as a band-aid to prevent home prices from falling any further. It seemed to many that bad behavior was being rewarded. Many argued preventing a full correction in prices would merely kick the can down the road. Combined with a very loose monetary policy, the housing market would simply become over-bought once again. And that is indeed exactly what happened, with home prices returning to previous bubble values within a decade. An unintended consequence is a massive transfer of wealth as younger generations are denied the opportunity to build home equity as a result of over-valued homes. Boomers are the beneficiaries in terms of out-sized realized gains, the result of years of financial repression.

We have seen federal programs target low-income households in the form of help with rent vouchers, and grants to states and local governments to use as they see fit. Assistance for homeownership has come in the form of mortgage interest tax deductions and mortgage insurance. For almost a century it's clear government involvement at both the federal, state, and local levels has played an impactful role in housing. What remains to be answered is how much of it was positive, and how much was poorly conceived.

For the most part, government involvement has been well-meaning, if not net-positive, especially in bringing about more equitable outcomes for those on lower incomes. However, in the aftermath of the 2009 crisis, cracks have remained in the housing market, and although governments may not have led the charge, they certainly haven't been complacent. Apart from obvious social and political reasons, it can be argued the government's primary motivation to remain engaged in housing is economic.

Housing and the Economy
The real estate market amounted to 18% of GDP in 2023, so contributes more to the economy than just about any other industry. Housing also contributes to employment and is a boost to affiliated industries such as furniture, renovations, and professional services. It is also an important source of revenue for local governments. Higher home prices mean higher property tax revenue, which it may be argued creates a conflict of interest. Maintaining price stability should be a government priority, but when that threatens tax revenues and economic output priorities change. It is rare to hear governments saying prices need to decline. It is much more common to hear plans to ease problems of high prices with solutions that involve debt and taxes. When home prices

reach lofty levels over an extended period, too much is at stake to allow that trend to reverse.

It's not only tax revenues and the economy that suffer. Homeowners also suffer from the effects of lost equity. The question is how long can massive equity gains be sustained when prices have created an affordability crisis? The irony is that while tax revenues increase as property values go up, tax credits may then be necessary to support those valuations. Increases in property taxes are often cited as a reason so many sellers don't want to sell their homes. This depletes supply and pushes up home prices. It's a vicious cycle.

Property taxes increase the cost burden to homeowners. They can also become inequitable and unevenly distributed. Prop 13 in California rewards long-term residents and penalizes newcomers. This is because property taxes are not based on the ability to pay, but on the value of the home. And home values are based on recent sales. When the cost to borrow increases and home values don't correct, the cost burden can be considerable as many first-time buyers can attest to. By preventing home prices from falling with stimulus such as tax credits, it's hard to see how the problem induced by over-valuations goes away. In this sense, governments are complicit in helping create volatility in house prices.

History Repeats Itself
In May of 2024, the Wall Street Journal, in its article "Return of the Housing Godzillas", reported that GSE

Freddie Mac was proposing to guarantee second mortgages to allow homeowners to release equity in their homes without sacrificing the low rate of their original mortgage. Current mortgage rates would only apply to the second, smaller mortgage. Borrowers would also be able to merge other consumer debt at the lower rate. This was proposed at a time when the mortgage business had dried up due to higher borrowing costs. The plan was to boost the mortgage industry as homeowners released the massive home equity build-up into the economy via consumption. This kind of plan has implications for borrowers who may not yet have built up any equity. If home prices fall it increases the risk of default and foreclosure. Systemic risk also increases as consumer debt consolidation degrades the credit quality on lenders' balance sheets. Once again we see solutions to a problem largely created by debt being sought in debt markets. Aggregate debt piles up and the market becomes over-leveraged raising the risk of defaults.

The amount of money tied up in home equity is very large. Much of this equity is the result of over-inflated prices. It is paper wealth. Since homes are a very illiquid and singular asset class, equity can only be released by selling the entire home. Borrowing against equity does not release equity in a true sense, since it simultaneously increases the homeowner's liabilities. This increase in liabilities affects the health of an individual's balance sheet by increasing the debt burden and in turn the risk of default. This is an example of governmental meddling, albeit indirectly, in the housing market the consequences of which could be detrimental to both homeowners and the broader economy.

In another article by the Wall Street Journal, entitled "Here Comes Kamala's Mortgage Forgiveness", the author lays bare the consequences of government tinkering at the fiscal level. These types of measures are reminiscent of those taken in 2009, which many believe contributed to the housing crisis back then. The justification for these interventions will no doubt be made on the basis that the housing market in 2024, doesn't face the same perils as in 2009. Lenders are better capitalized to withstand a shock, and borrowers are subject to much more credit scrutiny. In the latter case, this may not be entirely true. Whatever the case, it would appear the government is taking a gamble that it can contain things should matters devolve in the housing market.

Short-termism and expediency are the utensils of governments. Pre-emptive fiscal measures as opposed to reactive ones may signal a government alert to dangers that lie ahead. However, they can create their own sets of risks. The most contentious of Kamala Harris' proposals comes in the form of $25,000 in downpayment assistance to qualifying borrowers. This is aimed at mitigating the effects on the housing market of large home price increases. Since home prices are so high, down payments are also high and this creates a barrier to many buyers, especially first-time buyers. This measure will increase demand in an already supply-starved market. That in turn will put further upward pressure on home prices, propelling them to dangerously new highs. The higher home prices go, the further they have to fall, imperiling those very borrowers the measures were designed to assist.

Further evidence of potentially hasty government meddling comes from the FHA. Its measures are designed to help homeowners reduce the risk of losing their homes by assisting with late payments on mortgages. GSEs are similarly helping with mortgage payments for borrowers under financial pressure such as lost income and high property taxes. GSEs are also facilitating mortgage down payments are low as 3%, at the same time as lending standards have been lowered. Similarly, the FHA underwrites borrowers with down payments as low as 3.5%. If that wasn't enough, the 43% total debt hurdle above which lenders don't lend no longer applies to government-backed mortgages. That is precariously comparable to what happened in the last housing crisis.

As with Harris' proposals, borrowers are exposed to a greater risk of default and foreclosure because of the likely upward pressure on home prices these measures will have. The WSJ article further claims current delinquencies fall mostly to those with good credit scores and that those credit scores don't stand up to scrutiny for various reasons relating to other government debt forgiveness measures. Debt forgiveness, backstops, and mortgage assistance send a 'risk on' message to everyone thus fomenting moral hazard. If borrowers have been allowed to take on too much debt they are more exposed to default risk. If they have no skin in the game they have less incentive to meet their liabilities under financial pressure. Escalating and unsustainable prices with high levels of debt set the stage for an unraveling at some point. The more these elements are encouraged to run, the greater the damage of an eventual unwinding. If in the short-term we avoid the worst, it is likely the problem has been pushed off into the future rather than solved.

While governments have long been involved in housing, more recent decades show their role has become more strongly linked to credit markets and the economy than to one of social support. This is driven by the importance of real estate to both the economy and to consumers. However, the growth in importance has created unevenness in the distribution of that wealth. Homeownership rates are declining, homelessness is increasing, while financial burdens mount. Many can only dream of being a homeowner and building intergenerational wealth. For those fortunate enough to be able to buy a home in more recent years, the opportunity to build equity is diminished as high prices have resulted in a transfer of wealth to boomers. These are all symptoms of spiraling housing costs, a problem that governments remain reluctant to tackle head-on, preferring instead to skirt around the edges with expedient quick fixes, which are infused with the same genes that caused the problems in the first place.

However, unpalatable allowing, or even encouraging home prices to find a floor may be, it is the side of the price equation that would have a more lasting beneficial effect on the market as a whole. When Jerome Powell, the chairman of the Federal Bank in the US, announced drastic inflation-fighting monetary tightening, the consensus was among economists home prices would decline, as indeed they did, but only briefly. This was a welcome, and some say long overdue action, but one that fell foul of the unintended consequences of its own making. Years of accommodative policy and increased asset values, followed by a swift and dramatic central bank reversal brought about behavioral paralysis. Homeowners found themselves in the improbable position of being unable to afford to sell despite huge increases in property values. The Federal Reserve Bank enjoys some level of independence from the government, but its operations are largely harmonized with the goals of the government. Like the government, it also bears some responsibility for helping create the housing crisis.

Chapter 6

A little math every day keeps the sheriff at bay.

In previous chapters, we've looked at many aspects of the housing market in search of answers to questions about its general health. We examined the effects of monetary policy, valuation methods, information asymmetry, conflicts of interest, NIMBY-ism, consumer behavior, and government intervention. This chapter will look at macro and micro factors useful in analyzing real estate. The macro level looks at the fundamentals such as the economy, while the micro level is more about the technicals such as sales, inventory, and prices. For anyone deciding to buy, sell, or invest in real estate, having a working knowledge of the fundamentals and technicals is essential. We'll look at timing and whether this can be used to optimize decisions regarding home transactions. We'll also look at buy and sell considerations, and rent versus buys decisions.

Cycles

Our lives revolve around cycles of one kind or another. The seasonal cycle is one we are all familiar with. The business or economic cycle is another, which also affects our lives. Economies expand and contract with peaks and troughs marking the transition from one direction the economy takes to the other. There has been much debate over the years about the duration of economic cycles. Various theorists have offered profoundly different durations, based on different types of events being measured. Most recent research suggests cycles are random so don't easily fit into neat periodic ranges. Whatever their duration, most of us will have experienced more than one cycle in our lifetimes. The stock market cycle falls more or less in line with the business cycle but with a lag. As business earnings decrease from a slowing economy stock prices tend to fall. However, it is thought this has as much to do with 'fear' of investor returns. When it comes to the real estate market, however, there is some evidence the cycles are more deterministic.

One theory claims the real estate cycle is 18 years in duration. The cycle starts with a recovery from the end of the previous cycle. This is when land is at its cheapest. Population growth increases demand for goods and services aided by a lowering of interest rates, which stimulates demand. Companies expand, which increases the demand for land and real estate and soaks up existing supply. This leads to higher rents and attracts more investments in land development until supply satisfies demand. However, the long lead times for the development of land due to research, negotiations, permits, financing, and construction means there's inevitably a lag between supply and demand.

During the lag period expansion of the economy is fully underway putting upward price pressure on real estate. This upward pressure builds as investors believe future growth projections justify the increases in land values. As the new inventory eventually materializes, supply exceeds demand, and rents decline. Inflationary pressures in the broader economy due to the expansion lead to higher interest rates to cool things down. This increases developers' borrowing costs and bites into their margins. As the economy slows, the real estate market cools and goes into a decline. The rest is history.

This cycle has been measured going as far back as 1800. If the cycle's predictive powers are as robust as its proponents claim, 2025, or soon after should see a downturn start to happen in real estate in the US, which will last until the latter part of the decade. Apparently, the final phase of this real estate cycle is always followed by a recession. As of mid-2024, no leading indicators are screaming a decline in real estate prices or even an imminent recession.

While the theory of an 18-year cycle seems plausible, there are a few things it doesn't take into account.

Firstly, it is only in the last two decades that any significant changes in home prices are visible. This doesn't disclaim the existence of previous cycles, it just makes them somewhat overshadowed by the most recent cycle, which has demonstrated very observable changes in standard deviation. The theory also revolves around commercial real estate and land values, whereas residential real estate may be affected by different factors. For example, residential real estate is not subject to the same rigorous investment criteria as commercial real estate. Therefore, decisions to buy and sell won't follow the same economic path. Secondly, new homes are only ever a small percentage of total inventory, so over-supply as a result of lags in new homes coming to market won't be the only consideration driving the cycle. Moreover, supply problems may have their origins in other things. For example, we have already discussed how zoning regulations and NIMBY-ism restrict developers from building much-needed new homes. This is especially harmful as the effects become compounded over extended periods.

The theory also doesn't explain either the 'lock-in' effect of a sudden rise in mortgage rates, or other behavioral traits that shape decisions to sell, and which have serious consequences for supply. While cycles are useful for giving some indication of what we can expect going forward, there are other indicators worth exploring that help build a picture of the direction of the real estate market.

Technical Analysis

The most prescient of indicators for most asset classes is 'price'. What we mean by that is the direction in which price is traveling; up, down, or flat. The three main statistical methods for determining real estate prices are the average, the median, and repeat sales. There are pros and cons to them all. The average can become skewed if there are outliers in the data. The median simply informs about the middle data point, so doesn't say what's happening in other percentiles. The average and median will mostly track each other. If the average and median diverge, then the median is the better indicator. The repeat sale price calculation is considered by many to be the most accurate gauge of price movement because it uses the current and previous sales prices of homes.

The widely used index that uses the repeat sale formula is the Case Shiller House Price Index, which originated in academia but is now controlled by the rating agency Standard and Poor. The major drawback with this index is it lags by about three months, so data is never current. It also averages the last three months of data so actual monthly data is lost. The median price is published by the NAR and available on their website. Listing services such as Redfin and Zillow also publish their own median prices but with smaller lags. Lags are not as much of an issue with real estate as with financial products because prices are less volatile.

Once a trend in real estate prices is established, momentum and direction are consistent. There isn't much that derails momentum until it has played itself out. The bottom of the cycle may not be fully recognized until a reverse trend has been established. The rule of thumb is a period of three or more months indicates a trend. The steeper the curve the more significant the price direction. A steeply inclining curve may indicate prices have entered an irrational exuberance stage of a bubble. The inverse may indicate a bubble has burst. Conventional wisdom says the best time to buy is when the price curve has bottomed and is signaling a recovery. Equally, the worst time to buy is when prices have reached a top and are signaling downward momentum.

Leading indicators are useful in judging when the turning point in prices is about to occur. Sales volume is one such indicator. If sales are declining it means the market is cooling but won't yet be reflected in prices. Other indicators include the sales-to-list ratio and the percentage of homes selling above the list price. When the majority of homes sell below the list price, buyers are challenging list prices. A ratio in the mid to high 90% range is considered a balanced market.

Two other useful forward-looking indicators are DOMs (days-on-market) and the percentage of homes with price reductions. The longer a home sits without attracting offers, the more likely a price reduction will occur. Multiple price reductions indicate a distressed sale, which may present an opportunity for buyers to get a good deal. When the percentage of homes with price reductions is well into the double digits it may indicate prices are starting to turn downwards. Over 25% of homes with price reductions favor a buyer's market. These data can be found on listing services such as Redfin and Zillow. The NAR also makes some of this information publicly available.

Other leading indicators that don't use price as the main metric are related to mortgage payments. Delinquencies, defaults, and foreclosures are the three stages, in that order, indicating a borrower is struggling with meeting his, or her loan payments, or in the latter case has lost their home. Higher rates of delinquencies lead to higher defaults and ultimately foreclosures. Knowing when delinquencies are rising is more useful for leading indicator timing whereas the rate of foreclosures is a lagging indicator. Foreclosures can provide opportunities for finding deals below the current market price but they carry some risk. The condition of the property is not always publicized, so buyers don't always know what they are getting. When the percentage of borrowers struggling to meet monthly payments increases markedly, a market downturn or even a crash may be on the way. This would not necessarily be an opportune time to buy since it indicates the early stages of a property market decline. Higher default and foreclosure rates are more certain indicators for a market already in a downturn.

Inventory, or month's supply measures how long it would take to sell current listings at the prevailing sales rate. It is a useful indicator because it tells us whether we're in a buyer's or seller's market. The benchmark for when supply and demand are in balance—as far as it is possible to determine—is six months. Anything below this number is indicative of a seller's market so we can expect prices to be 'sticky', or rising. Using the median price index and the sale-to-list ratio will confirm this trend. If inventory builds, or is already high this encourages buyers to challenge the list price to seek a better deal for themselves. Inventory could be rising because sellers are panicking and want to sell to cash in gains. It could also indicate home sales are slowing so sitting for longer, which can be verified by looking at the number of days (DOMs) it takes to sell homes. A contraction in supply increases prices, and expanding supply puts downward pressure on prices. It comes as no surprise the best to sell is in a seller's market and the best time to haggle on price is in a buyer's market. There are buyers and sellers in every market and generally speaking, these guiding principles are not always apparent to consumers.

The above technical indicators presuppose it is possible to 'time the market'. Buyers and sellers are attempting to get the best deals they can by buying or selling at the most favorable time. However, the best time to buy is not always the best time to sell, which explains why some buyers and sellers will 'sit on the fence' waiting for a more opportune time. When this happens it can be a drag on supply and sales. In financial markets, there is substantial evidence it is not possible to time the market. Housing is different because of the long time it takes to sell a home and the tendency for price trends to continue. There are exceptions to this rule as in 2023, when home prices had been falling but reversed confounding expectations about what many thought should be happening. For the most part, indicators are reliable tools to use when attempting to time the market. However, on their own they have less usefulness and, therefore need to be used in conjunction with fundamental analysis, which involves macro events like interest rate policy and the economy. For example, recessions and housing market declines are inextricably linked.

Fundamental Analysis
Having explored the dynamics of the housing market at the micro level using technical analysis, we'll now turn our attention to macro factors to gain a better understanding of the big picture. This is sometimes referred to as fundamental analysis. Understanding the basics of how the housing market is interconnected with the economy is a prerequisite for maximizing decision-making. All things being equal, a healthy economy usually results in a healthy housing market. A healthy housing market is likewise good for the economy. Markers for a good economy are stable growth as measured by GDP (gross domestic product), unemployment in the range of 3.5% to 4.5%, and inflation hovering around 2%.

GDP is the total net output of an economy. It comprises consumption, investment, government spending, and exports minus imports. When there are two consecutive quarters of negative GDP growth, the economy is considered to be in a technical recession.

When the economy is expanding consumers are more confident, which is good for housing. Consumer sentiment indices are good indicators of the current state of the economy. Consumers spend more when they feel good about the economy and their finances. As the economy contracts, unemployment increases and with it the difficulties meeting major costs such as mortgage payments.

At the beginning of this chapter of the book, we talked about the economic cycle. This has important implications for housing because of changes in the yield curve that track changes in the economic cycle. The yield curve shows a snapshot of yields over a range of maturities of government bonds. It is a predictor of the direction of interest rates, the economy, and mortgage rates. The curve is shaped by the difference between yields of shorter and longer maturities and is normally upward-sloping, meaning longer-term bonds have higher yields than shorter-term bonds. When the curve inverts longer term yields are lower than short term yields. This is because investors have a pessimistic view of the economy going forward. The inverted yield curve has an almost infallible record for predicting recessions.

House prices tend to fall as a result of recessions. Interest rates are lowered in downturns to help stimulate the economy. That means mortgage rates will also come down, but that won't help home buyers if job security is at risk. So timing the market can be a double-edged sword. It has both benefits and risks. Risks are compounded when both interest rates and home prices are high. This is not a good time to buy a home, especially when recession indicators such as an inverted yield curve are flashing red. However, a healthy economy combined with a limited supply of homes for sale counter these downward pressures, such as in 2024. The conventional wisdom suggests excessively high valuations are not sustainable, and corrections may be triggered by the low point of inexorable economic cycles.

Any planning involves some speculation about what may happen in the future. Buying a home depends on personal finances, which are subject to exogenous factors, especially the economy. There is no crystal ball for replicating the future, but there are other leading economic indicators (LEIs) besides those mentioned above, which help ascertain the likely direction of the economy. These indicators look at specific areas of the economy such as managers' orders, sales, housing permits, spending, and even the performance of the stock market. Fortunately, many of these are brought together into a single measure by The Conference Board, a not-for-profit think-tank with membership drawn from a large pool of businesses. A wide range of economic indicators is condensed into one or two easily digestible paragraphs highlighting where economic strengths and weaknesses lie and the likelihood of a recession.

Since buying (and selling) a home is the biggest financial decision most of make, it is prudent to place the decision into a broader context and not just base it on personal and emotional factors. Examining microdata within the macroeconomic framework better informs decision-making. Understanding how home prices may be impacted by interest rate changes is fundamental to informed decision-making. Being aware of the interplay between technicals and economic cycles helps in achieving goals. Is the goal to build wealth through home equity? How likely is that achievable when home prices are soaring? If economic indicators point towards a slowing economy, is your personal financial situation secure enough to ride any storms, including keeping up with mortgage payments? Are government incentives and industry lending standards working in your best interests, or are they creating potential pitfalls for you down the road? Is buying a home the best option for your current situation?

Rent vs Buy
An alternative to buying a home is renting. The notion that renting is pouring money down the drain because it is paying someone else's mortgage is an industry myth perpetuated to goad people into buying. Renting has many clear advantages such as increased mobility, proximity to the workplace, and usually lower costs providing an opportunity to save and invest. Many online calculators will do the numerical heavy lifting for you when deciding to rent or buy. However, there is no substitute for doing the math yourself with the use of a calculator or spreadsheet. Easy traps to fall into are underestimating the true cost of home ownership.

The majority of first-time buyers fail to take into account rehabbing, insurance, property taxes, and maintenance. These costs can fluctuate considerably due to inflation, changing weather patterns, and inflated home prices. A back-of-cigarette packet calculation can help determine whether more thorough financial scrutiny is warranted. Multiply the comparable rent of the home you wish to buy by twelve to give annual numbers. Divide that number into the home price. If the number is greater than 20, it is generally better to rent than to buy. Any number below 20, favors buying over renting.

A worked example follows below:

$$\text{Monthly rent} = \$2,500$$

$$\$2,500 \times 12 \text{ month} = \$30,000$$

$$\text{Annual Rent} = \$30,000$$

$$\text{Home price} = \$500,000$$

$$\$500,000 \div \$30,000 = 16.67$$

$$\text{Buy vs rent ratio} = 16.67$$

In the above example, a ratio of 16.67 appears to favor buying a home over renting. However, it is good practice to compare the results with other sources. Finally, there is no social stigma attached to renting, which carries none of the stresses associated with home ownership such as burdensome costs and concerns.

Epilogue

The book's premise is based on the idea that something is not quite right with the housing market. There are forces at play that have been distorting prices putting home ownership out of reach for an increasing number of people. It is important to gain an understanding of these issues if we are to avoid the turmoil that resulted from the 2006 housing bubble and the severe recession in the few short years that followed. The impact was felt globally and lingered well into the future. The past is never a predictor of the future but should act to remind us of what can happen when the stars are similarly aligned. It should also teach us that making similar mistakes won't magically result in different outcomes.

A deeper look under the bonnet of housing has shown that several factors contribute to our housing woes. When we see similar housing crises arising around the world against a similar backdrop, it confirms the leading causes. Very accommodative monetary policy has pushed up values of all asset classes, including real estate, and has social consequences, most notably homelessness. It also creates an affordability crisis that has far-reaching financial consequences for future generations. An over-valued housing market also has broader implications for the economy as a whole. Unsustainable prices and high levels of debt will test the fragility of the housing market, highlighting the pitfalls we too easily succumb to.

Focussing on things that have proportionately less impact on housing is not useful. Lobbying power, information asymmetry, and inherent conflicts of interest within the industry merit closer examination. Valuation methods need revising as they often only serve to exacerbate problems. Government responses to problems in housing are often reactive and based on political expediency. Measures to stimulate housing, or put a floor under falling prices often make matters worse because they push the problem down the road, or create moral hazard. Zoning regulations and NIMBY-ism seriously exacerbate supply issues.

Before we lay all the blame at the industry's and government's feet, let us not forget consumer behavior plays a pivotal role in housing crises. That may be in part because consumers remain largely uninformed, but it is also because emotions get in the way of rational choices. This can be remedied by creating awareness of self-deception and monitoring external factors that help inform and improve decision-making thus minimizing regret.

Useful Websites (active links digital version)

Economy
https://www.bea.gov/
https://www.census.gov/economic-indicators/
https://www.gapminder.org/
https://www.worldbank.org/
https://www.imf.org/external/index.htm
https://www.ons.gov.uk/
https://data.london.gov.uk/

Indicators
https://www.conference-board.org/data/bci.cfm
https://www.bls.gov/
https://fred.stlouisfed.org/
https://www.consumeraffairs.com/finance/mortgage-delinquency-rate-trends.html

Housing Data
https://www.redfin.com/blog/data-center/
https://www.redfin.com/blog/real-estate-news/
https://www.zillow.com/research/data/
https://www.nar.realtor/
http://www.acadata.co.uk/

Home Prices
https://fred.stlouisfed.org/series/csushpinsahttps://realestatedecoded.com/case-shiller/
https://www.gov.uk/search-house-prices
https://www.fhfa.gov/DataTools/Downloads/Pages/House-Price-Index.aspx

Affordability

https://www.nar.realtor/research-and-statistics/housing-statistics/housing-affordability-index

https://www.car.org/aboutus/mediacenter/newsreleases/2024-News-Releases/1qtr2024hai

https://www.census.gov/topics/housing/housing-affordability.html

https://www.atlantafed.org/center-for-housing-and-policy/data-and-tools/home-ownership-affordability-monitor

References

Alexander Hermann, Housing Perspectives, Harvard Joint Center for Housing Studies, September 2023

Ryan Jones, Cycles within the US and Real Estate Markets, Regions Asset Management, October 2020

Matt Christopherson, International Transactions in US Residential Real Estate, National Association of Realtors, 2023

Jane Dock, Housing Affordability: Recommendations for New Research to Guide Policy, Federal Reserve Bank Economic Policy Review 23, No. 3 December 2018

2024 Income and Affordability Study, New York City Rent Guidelines Board, April 2024

Affordability Index, National Association of Realtors, 2023

Housing Affordability: Local and National Perspectives, Laurie Goodman Urban Institute, Wei Li Federal Deposit Insurance Corporation, April 2018

Locked Out: Social Value Cost of GTA's Housing Crisis, Canadian Centre for Economic Analysis, January 2024

Agency MBS Purchase: Overview, History, Benefits, Investopedia, October 2023

Vanessa Brown Calder, Are Institutional Investors a Problem in the Housing Market? Cato Institute, November 2023

Agostino Valier, Ezio Micelli, Automated Models for Value Prediction: A Critical Review of the Debate, Valori e Valutazioni No 24, 2020

Diego Salzman, Remco Zwinkels, Behavioral Real Estate, Duisenberg School of Finance, July 2013

Jingyi Liu, Behavioral Biases in the Housing Market, University of Cambridge, October 2022

Akshita Singh et al, Behavioral Biases in Real Estate Investment, Humanities and Social Sciences Communications, November 2023

Sanat Pat Raikar, Blalck Swan Event, Britannica, May 2024

California Housing Affordability Update, California Association of Realtors, 2024

Ben Uhler, California Housing Affordability Tracker, LAO Legislative Analyst's Office, April 2024

Veronica Dagher, Capital Gains Tax Hits More Home Sellers, Wall Street Journal, May 2024

Stephan Luck, Thomas Zimmerman, Ten Years Later: Did QE Work? Federal Reserve Bank of New York, May 2019

Josh Herrenkohl, Does Institutional Ownership of SFRs Help or Hurt the Housing Sector? Wealth Management.com, June 2022

Hanneke Van Deursen, The People's Housing: Woningcorporaties and Dutch Social Housing System, Joint Center for Housing Studies, Harvard University, June 2023

Melissa Dittman Tracey, Home Prices, Inventory Force Foreign Buyers to Retreat, National Association of Realtors, August 2023

Editorial Board, Return of the Housing Godzillas, Wall Street Journal, May 2924

Annie Lowry, Why Isn't the Government Doing More About the Housing Crisis?, The Atlantic Decade, 2023

Maggie McCarty et al, Overview of Federal Housing Assistance Programs and Policy, Congressional Research Service, March 2019

Will Parker, Harris Housing Plan Aims to Add Three Millions Homes. That Won't be Easy. Wall Street Journal, August 2024

State of the Nation's Housing 2023, Joint Center for Housing Studies of Harvard University, 2023

Paul Migliorato et al, Defining and Measuring Housing Affordability in the State of Hawaii, Department of Business, Economic Development and Tourism, February 2024

Alexander Hermann, Peyton Whitney, Home Price-to-Income Reaches Record High, Joint Center for Housing Studies, Harvard University, January 2024

2023 Annual Homelessness Assessment Report, US Department of Housing and Urban Development, December 2023

Ferdi Botha et al, Housing Affordability Stress and Mental health, Australian Economic Papers, February 2024

The Importance of Housing Affordability and Stability for Preventing and Ending Homelessness, US Interagency Council on Homelessness, May 2019

Benjamin Keys, How Foreign Purchases of US Homes Impact Prices and Supply, Wharton School of University of Pennsylvania, September 2020

Clark Merrefield, How Neighborhoods Fare When Institutional Investors Buy Single Family Homes, the Journalist's Resource, February 2023

Jane Ihrig, Scott Wolla, How Does the Fed Influence Rates Using Its New Tools? Federal Reserve Bank of St Louis, August 2020

Teo Nicolais, Hot to Use Real Estate Trends to Predict the Next Housing Bubble, Harvard Extension School, October 2016

Sumit Agarwal et al, Do Real Estate Agents Have Information Advantages in Housing Markets? Journal of Financial Economics, December 2019

US Governmental Accountability Office, Rental Housing: Information on Institutional Investment in Single Family Homes, May 2924

Office of Policy Development and Research, Institutional Investors in Housing, January 2023

Will Parker, Wall Street Has Spent Billions Buying Homes, Wall Street Journal, April 2024

Ross Batzer et al, The Lock-In Effect of Rising Mortgage Rates. Federal Housing Federal Agency (FHFA), March 2024

Moody's, Key Risk Factors In Securitization of Single Family Rental Properties, August 2012

Allysia Finley, Here Comes Kamala's Mortgage Forgiveness, Wall Street Journal, August 2024

Laura Kusisto, Nicole Friedman, Realtors are in Crisis: Home Buyers Could be the Winners, Wall Street Journal, February 2024

Debra Kamin, The Homeowners Who Beat the National Association of Realtors, New York Times, March 2024

Andy Markowitz, Are the Last Boomers Ready for Retirement? AARP, April 2024

Wikipedia, Quantitative Easing

National Association of Realtors, Real Estate's Impact on the Economy by the Numbers, May 2024

Editorial Board, Realtors face Antitrust Reckoning, Wall Street Journal, October 2023

Daniel Shaw, David Moore, Realtors' Lobby Plows Political Cash into Efforts to Keep Rents Higher, More Perfect Union, November 2022

Roof Online, Relative Construction Costs by US State, 2024

Federal Reserve Bank of Atlanta, Are Single Family Rental Securitizations Here to Stay? May 2014

Bill Conroy, As Rates Skyrocket, Wall Street Single Family Rental Investors See Opportunity, Housingwire, June 2022

Steve Hanke, The Great 18-Year Real Estate Cycle, Cato Institute, January 2010

Lily Geismer, America Needs a New Approach to Affordable Housing, Time Magazine, March 2024

Matt Brannon, The True Cost of Homeownership, Real Estate Witch, March 2024

National Association of Realtors, The Truth About the NAT Settlement Agreement, Realtor Magazine, March 2024

US Federal Reserve System, The Fed Explained, Public Education and Outreach, 11th edition, August 2021

Paul Tastevin, Charlotte Ruston, Global Real Estate Universe in Comparison, Savill's Research, September 2023

Richard Fry et al, US Household Growth Over Last Decade, Pew Research Center, October 2021

Treh Manhertz, US Housing Market has Doubled in Value, Zillow, January 2022

Emily Peck, What Happens When You Give People Money to Buy Houses, Axios, April 2024

Jaclyn DeJohn, Where the Most New Construction Homes Are Being Added, Smart Asset, May 2024

Manuela Tobias et al, California: Here's Why Your Housing Costs Are High, Cal Matters, August 2017

Eric Wallerstein, Young Americans Are Getting Left Behind by Rising Home Prices, Wall Street Journal, April 2024

Bloomberg News, World's Bubbliest Housing Markets Are Flashing Warning Signs, July 2022

Index

Affordability 14
Affordability index 42, 80
AI (Artificial Intelligence) 75
Algorithms..75, 89
Anchoring bias 77, 91
Appraisers 69, 74
Automated Valuation Models (AVMs) 75
Behavioral biases..90
Behavioral finance 88
Bidding wars 15, 94
Buyer's market...65, 74, 120
California Association of Realtors (CAR) 15, 79
CAPM (Capital Assets Pricing Model) 71
CAR affordability index 80
Case Shiller Home Price Index......................11, 23, 64, 118
Commercial real estate 8, 73, 117
Comparable prices......................................56, 67, 90
Comps..56, 68, 90
Confirmation bias...89
Conflicts of interest 56, 114
Cost of land 38
Cost to build 38, 53, 67
COVID-19..10, 23, 42
DCF (discounted cash flow)..70
Debt forgiveness 110
Default risk 29, 67, 96
Defaults 49, 108, 120
Delinquencies...110, 120
Demographics...8, 41
Developers 39, 103, 116
Discount rate 70
Discrimination..103

137

Dodd-Frank Act 104
DOMs (days-on-market) 119
Economic cycles 115, 124
Endowment Effect 97
Fannie Mae and Freddie Mac 24
Federal Funds Rate 26
Federal government 102
Federal Reserve Bank 13, 25, 93
First-time buyers (FTBs) 37, 105, 125
Fiscal policies 97
Foreclosures 7, 34, 45
Foreign Buyers 50
Freddie Mac 24, 108
Fundamental Analysis 122
Fundamental Valuation 70
Fundamentals 71, 114
GDP (Gross Domestic Product) 122
Gentrification 41, 95
Gordon Growth Model 72
Government incentives 87, 125
Great Depression 101
Great Recession 104
GRM (Gross Rent Multiplier) 73
GSEs (Government Sponsored Entities) 24, 45
Herding 93
Heuristics 91
HOA fees 37
Homelessness 44, 111
Homeowners Affordability and Stability Plan 33
Housing and Urban Development (HUD) 44, 102
Housing bubble 7, 27, 94
Housing Indicators 65
Institutional Investors 45

Insurance costs 37
Interest rate 6, 13, 22
Intergenerational wealth 24, 111
Intrinsic value 74, 79, 83
Inventory 17, 120
Irrational exuberance 93, 119
Jerome Powell 112
Leading economic indicators (LEIs) 124
List-to-sales ratio 65
Loan-to-value LTV 19
MBSs (mortgage-backed securities) 13, 27
Median income 16, 34, 80
Median price 14, 57, 79
MLS (Multiple Losing Service) 59
Model of valuation 72
Monetary easing 25
Monetary policy 24, 27, 87
Months supply 17, 65
Moral hazard 34, 42, 61
Morningstar 62, 76
National Association of Realtors (NAR) 59
Information asymmetry 8, 56, 114
NIMBY-ism 53, 114
NOI (net operating income) 74
Over-Confidence 94
Over-optimism 95
Price reductions 65, 119
Prop 13 107
Property taxes 37, 107
Public Housing 103
Quantitative Easing (QE) 28
Real estate cycle 115
Recession 22, 65, 104

Redfin 17, 65, 77
Regulations 87, 117
Repeat sales 12, 64, 118
Sales 22, 65
Sales volume 119
SEC (Securities and Exchange Commission) 62
Section 8 103
Self-attribution 95
Self-deception 94
Short-termism 29, 109
Stimulus bill 104
Systemic risk 49, 108
Technical analysis 118
The Conference Board 22, 124
Unemployment 27, 66, 122
Valuation 56, 66, 71
Value 25, 30, 54
Volatility 63, 107
Yield curve 123
Zillow 65, 75, 80

www.ingramcontent.com/pod-product-compliance
Lightning Source LLC
Chambersburg PA
CBHW052302220526
45471CB00001B/455